VOGUE® KNITTING
The Ultimate Hat Book

VOGUE® KNITTING

The Ultimate Hat Book

history • technique • design

THE EDITORS OF VOGUE® KNITTING MAGAZINE

sixth&springbooks
NEW YORK

sixth&spring books

161 Avenue of the Americas, New York, NY 10013

Editorial Director JOY AQUILINO	Instructions Editors LISA BUCCELLATO PAT HARSTE LORI STEINBERG	Vice President, Publisher TRISHA MALCOLM
Senior Editor MICHELLE BREDESON		Creative Director JOE VIOR
Art Director DIANE LAMPHRON	Instructions Proofreaders CHARLOTTE PARRY JUDITH SLOAN	Production Manager DAVID JOINNIDES
Yarn Editor CHRISTINA BEHNKE	Technical Illustrations ULI MONCH	President ART JOINNIDES
Stylist KHALIAH JONES	Hair and Makeup SOKPHALLA BAN USING SONIA KASHUK MAKEUP	

PHOTO CREDITS
All photography by Rose Callahan, excepted as noted below:

Page 9: photos from 1947, 1949, and 1951 by Fred Baker (©Condé Nast Publications, Inc); photo from 1968 by Tom Palumbo (©Condé Nast Publications, Inc)

Pages 39-40: Paul Amato for LVARepresents.com

Page 52: Paul Amato LVARepresents.com

Page 78: Marcus Tullis

Page 126: Paul Amato LVARepresents.com

Page 128: Paul Amato LVARepresents.com

Page 148: Paul Amato LVARepresents.com

ISBN: 978-1-936096-50-3

Library of Congress Control Number: 2012941914

MANUFACTURED IN CHINA

1 3 5 7 9 10 8 6 4 2

First Edition

Contents

Hats Off *to* Knitting!

Growing up in hot and sunny Australia, warm hats were not a fundamental part of my wardrobe, and it wasn't until I was seventeen and on a school trip to actually see snow that I began to appreciate their virtues. Experiencing my first New York winter years later, I was convinced! Nothing feels cozier on a chilly day than a warm hat.

In *Vogue Knitting The Ultimate Hat Book*, we celebrate the hat. From snug beanies that keep out the chill to frothy fascinators that make headlines (pun intended) at royal weddings, hats are an integral part of any wardrobe and have stood the fashion test of time. Hats are probably the second most popular item to knit (a close runner-up to scarves), and it's easy to see why. A hat not only warms the head, it can also brighten your outfit and mood. Hats are great gifts to knit, because while fit is important, it's not as crucial for hats as for sweaters. Many hats take only one or two skeins of yarn, making them economical and a good way to use up your stash. For beginners who want to try a new technique for the first time but don't want to bite off more than they can knit, a hat is ideal. And more experienced stitchers can experiment with new techniques without fear of commitment.

To create this collection, we combed through the *Vogue Knitting* archives in search of our favorite and most enduring head coverings. We then sent out a call to our designers to create their perfect hat. Without giving them any further parameters, we received a staggering variety of original ideas. From these we chose the hats that best represent the most popular knit hat styles, often with a new spin, as well as caps that push the boundaries of hat design.

Whether you're looking for practicality or style, a quick-and-easy knit or a technical challenge, you'll find plenty of hats that fit the bill. We hope you enjoy this book as much as we've enjoyed creating it!

Trisha Malcolm
Editorial Director, *Vogue Knitting*

History of Knitted Hats

Hats have been worn since ancient times. A Thebes tomb painting of a man wearing a straw hat is the oldest known image of a hat. Although the history of knitted hats is probably not quite as long, it is a rich one.

It's unknown when the first hat was knit, but the oldest surviving examples of knitted garments were felted caps, stockings, and sleeve pieces. The so-called Monmouth cap, a felted knit hat, was first produced in the 13th century in Coventry, England, and a version of it was still being made in the 19th century for soldiers to wear in the Crimean War. The earliest cap knitters were licensed by the government and their prices were controlled to prevent profiteering. Their tools—knitting needles—were difficult to manufacture and therefore both scarce and precious.

At the beginning of the 17th century, better metalworking techniques allowed for the production of uniform knitting needles. This led to the development of knitting guilds, some of which survived well into the 18th century. Exclusively male and intensely competitive, the guilds (the earliest of which were for cap knitters) required a long and elaborate apprenticeship. An aspiring master knitter had to produce a felted cap and several other pieces.

Several examples of knitted hats from the 1700s survive in museum collections, including a silk cap with a tassel from Spain and a loose-fitting knitted or crocheted cap with earflap-like extensions.

As demand for knitted products grew, the craft spread. Skilled tradesmen produced fine knitted items, but in the countryside a cruder form of the craft was taking shape. Knitting was easy to learn, transport, and pick up or put down at any given moment, and farmers, fishmongers, and shepherds began producing caps, as well as socks and stockings, both to clothe their families and to sell at market.

The rise of the Industrial Age brought an end to the handknitting industry, though it still held on as a means of supplemental income in some rural areas. Knitting by hand, which before had been viewed as a lower-class pursuit (ladies of position embroidered or did other fine needlework), became a leisure activity of the middle class. Improvements were made in mass-produced yarns, and the availability of pattern books and magazines spread. The 19th century also saw the rise of many folk knitting traditions. Knitting became a means of improving prospects for the poor, and knitting cooperatives were established to preserve native handcraft and provide a means of self-sustenance in the British Isles, Sweden, Canada, and South America.

In the Andean region of South America, for example, knitted hats are an important part of the culture. Knitting was likely introduced to the Andes by the Spanish and Portuguese, but the indigenous peoples adapted the craft to their own traditions, creating caps and leggings that replicate their woven clothing. The intricately patterned tasseled knit caps, or chullos, are perhaps the most recognizable Andean designs.

Popular interest in knitting in America and Great Britain had dwindled by the 20th century, but World War I sparked a new surge in the craft. When America entered World War I in 1917, the American Red Cross launched massive nationwide volunteer knitting campaigns to supply soliders on the European front with warm clothing. Thousands of women stitched wool hats, socks, and sweaters from patterns that had been approved by the armed forces. World War II saw another rise in volunteer knitting, and Red Cross knitters continued to supply the military with wool hats as late as 1964. Soldiers stationed at remote outposts such as Greenland and Labrador claimed the wool hats were warmer than the mass-produced synthetic versions supplied by the army.

Knitted hat designs from the mid 20th century would not be out of place today. Popular looks from the *Vogue Knitting Book,* an earlier incarnation of *Vogue Knitting,* included stocking caps, watch caps, fitted "pixie" caps, balaclava-like hoods, and baby bonnets. Needles continued to click throughout the 1950s and '60s, but it wasn't until the late '70s and early '80s that popular interest in the craft again emerged, fueled in part by the amazing works of knitted color and pattern that began to appear in England.

Knitting came on bigger than ever in early 2000, thanks to the handknits that were paraded down fashion runways and A-list celebrities who gave knitting a glamorous profile. With the boom of blogs and social media, knitting continues to gain in popularity. Hats are perennial favorite projects to knit because they are suitable for all skill levels and knit up relatively quickly. Charity knitting is also alive and well, with numerous organizations collecting and distributing knitted items, including hats for preemies and other at-risk babies and "chemo caps" for cancer patients who have lost their hair. New books, yarns, patterns, and designers continue to feed our need to knit, confirming that knitted hats are here to stay. ■

Vogue® Knitting Then & Now

Hat designs from the 1940s, '50s, and '60s that appeared in the Vogue Knitting Book *share many of the same shapes as today's hats. (Patterns for today's hats, from top to bottom, are on pages 115, 150, 170, and 82.)*

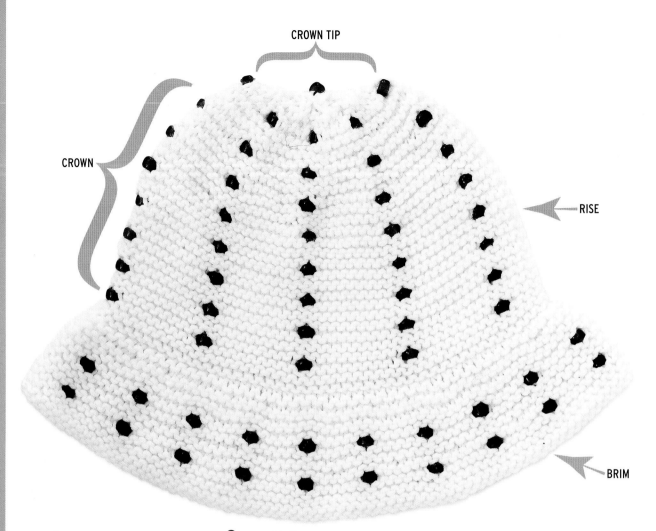

CROWN TIP

CROWN

RISE

BRIM

Anatomy of a Hat

At its most basic, a hat consists of a brim or band and a crown. Of course there are endless ways to vary the shape and size of these components, as well as other features some hats possess. Here are a few terms you'll encounter in this book.

Crown

The portion of a hat that covers the head is called the crown. The crown can vary in depth. A beanie, for example, has a shallow crown that hugs the head. A tuque features a deep crown that extends slightly beyond the top of the head. The portion of the crown that forms the sides of the hat is called the *rise,* while the top of the crown is often referred to as the *crown tip.*

Brim

The brim is the lower projecting portion of the hat. A brim can be shallow or wide, depending on the style. A cloche generally has a very shallow brim that is more prominent in the front. The brim of a bucket hat is evenly wide around the circumference of the hat and projects from one to several inches. A sun hat, designed to shade the face, has a very deep brim.

Band

Some hats, especially knit hats, simply have a narrow band around the base of the hat, rather than a projecting brim. The band of a knit hat is often worked in a rib pattern to be slightly smaller than the head circumference, allowing it to stretch to fit the wearer snugly. The beret shown at right (see page 31), for example, features a corrugated rib band. Knit bands generally range from one to two inches deep.

BAND

Cuff

If you knit the band to be double the desired width when worn, you can fold it back to form a cuff as in the Cabled Watch cap on page 80 (right). A cuff can add extra warmth as well as a design element. Because the "wrong" side of the cuff will show when folded back, you should knit the cuff in a stitch pattern that is reversible or plan ahead to knit the desired pattern on the wrong side. Like bands, cuffs are often knit in rib patterns for stretchability.

CUFF

Visor

A visor, or bill, is a favorite feature of sporty hats. Essentially an extension of the brim in the front of the hat, a visor provides extra shade for the face. A visor is created by knitting in a dense stitch pattern that is naturally rigid (as in the Brimmed Pompom Hat on page 67 and at right) or by sewing the brim to create a pocket into which a plastic or cardboard crescent is inserted (see, for example, the Bobbled Visor Hat on page 160).

VISOR

Earflaps

Earflaps can be knit as part of the body of the hat or stitched separately and attached. Earflaps are often finished with cords that tie around the chin. Chullos (such as the Tasseled Chullo at right; page 170) and trappers usually feature earflaps. In trappers, the earflaps often merge into a band that covers the back of the neck.

EARFLAPS

Types of Hats

This book features fifty hat designs, which fall into the following basic types. (The first chapter of patterns, Basic Shapes, features one of each type.) Of course there are many variations on the basic styles and some that don't fit neatly into a classic shape.

Beanie
The simplest type of knit hat, a beanie is a brimless hat that fits closely to the head. The finished circumference will be smaller than your actual head measurement so the beanie stretches. Beanies are usually stitched in the round from the bottom up, and are often striped or colorfully patterned.

Beret
Berets, or tams, are flat caps, often topped with a pompom or tassel. Since this style only has to fit the head around the band edge, the band is usually elastic enough to fit all sizes. When the band is completed, several stitches are increased in one or two rows or rounds. After several inches, decreases are worked at even intervals to form the signature flat shape.

Cloche
Named for the French word for "bell," the cloche became popular in the 1920s as women cut their hair shorter. A cloche fits fairly close to the head and has a shallow brim that turns down slightly. Although traditionally made of felt, cloches are popular knits and are often embellished with ribbon or knit flowers.

Pillbox Hat
Originally military-issue, the pillbox became part of mainstream fashion in the late 1950s and early '60s, thanks in part to Jackie Kennedy. Pillboxes are sleek, chic caps with straight sides and no brim. Knit pillboxes are often worked in two pieces, with the flat crown tip and straight sides knit separately and joined.

Bucket Hat
A bucket hat is a casual style that features a fairly deep brim that turns up slightly. Buckets hats are usually knit from the crown down; the brim can be a continuation of the crown or knit separately.

Watch Cap
Similar to a beanie with a deep cuff, this classic knit hat is usually worked in the round from the bottom up.

Bowler
A bowler is a traditional menswear style, featuring a rounded crown and turned-up brim. Felting gives a bowler extra stiffness and shape. A *fedora* is similar to a bowler with a less-rounded crown and shallower brim.

Stocking Cap
A stocking cap is elongated through very gradual decreases. A playful look, stocking caps often incorporate colorwork and/or a pompom at the tip.

Chullo
Originating in the Andes, a chullo is similar to a beanie with earflaps and is usually worked in stranded colorwork or intarsia. This collection features several chullos, which have become fashion basics.

Newsboy Cap
A newsboy cap, or *Gatsby,* is a style from the late 19th and early 20th centuries that features a flat cap and a visor. First worn by men and boys, the newsboy is now also popular with women.

Hood
The simplest knitted hood is a rectangle that has been seamed up the back, usually with added ties. A hood can be elongated to create a scarf. A *balaclava* is similar to a hood, but is extended to cover the throat and part of the face.

Paperbag Hat
One of the most basic hat styles, a paperbag hat is essentially a straight tube that is cinched at the top with a drawstring. Popular for children, they are also a whimsical and easy-to-knit look for adults.

Trapper
A trapper is a mountain man's hat that has found favor as stylish urban wear. Featuring a deep, turned-up brim and earflaps, or a band that extends to cover the back of the neck, a trapper is an extremely warm and cozy hat. Traditional trappers often feature fur linings.

Tuque
Also known as a *ski cap,* a tuque is a close-fitting, slightly elongated hat that tapers to a blunt point. It often has tassels attached to the crown and can feature a small visor.

BERET

CLOCHE

BOWLER

TRAPPER

TUQUE

TYPES OF HATS

13

Basic Techniques

Before we get in over our heads, let's take a moment to cover some issues that apply to knitting most hats, including construction methods and finishing techniques, choosing and substituting yarns, and tips for getting a good fit.

HAT CONSTRUCTION

There are several different common approaches to constructing a hat. Some are knit in one piece, while others are knit as two or more components that are then joined. Because most hats are round, knitting in the round is the most popular way to work them, but certain styles lend themselves to knitting flat back and forth. Brims are often knit back and forth, then continued in the round to form the crown, such as the cloche on page 55.

Knitting in the Round

Most hats are worked in the round with a circular needle, switching to double-pointed needles as the stitches decrease and no longer fit comfortably on the circular. Most of the hats in this book are worked by beginning at the lower band or brim edge and continuing up the sides, ending at the crown tip and leaving the last few stitches on the needles. After cutting the yarn, simply draw it through the remaining stitches twice and fasten off. Other hats are cast on at the crown tip on double-

pointed needles and worked down to the band or brim. This allows you to more easily adjust the depth and circumference of the hat to fit your head.

Knitting Back and Forth

While the majority of hats in this collection are knit in the round, several are worked back and forth, or flat, on straight needles. Hood-style hats, such as the Cabled Rib Hood on page 73, are often knit as flat rectangles, then seamed to create the hood shape. Other hats are knit back and forth with decreases in the crown for shaping, then seamed in the back. When a hat is knit flat, an invisible back seam should be sewn from the right side.

GAUGE

It is always important to knit a gauge swatch, and it is even more so with hats, as they are designed to fit securely. If your gauge is too loose, you could end up with your hat over your eyes; if it's too tight, the hat will perch oddly at the top of your head. Making a flat gauge swatch for hats knit in the

This cloche (page 129) is knit in the round starting with the brim and working up through the crown.

An easy way to make a hood like this one (page 73) is to knit a rectangle back and forth and seam it.

Knitting the brim back and forth and the crown in the round combines the best of both worlds (page 55).

Measuring stitch gauge with a tape measure.

Measuring row gauge with a tape measure.

Using a stitch gauge.

round will allow you to measure gauge over a 4"/10cm span that will lay flat for better reading. However, when a hat includes a complex stitch pattern knit in rounds, a circularly knit swatch will test the gauge best, and the practice will familiarize you with the pattern. The type of needles used—straight or circular, wood or metal—will also influence gauge, so knit your swatch with the needles you plan to use for the project. Measure gauge as shown on page 14. Try different needle sizes until your sample measures the required number of stitches and rows. To get fewer stitches to the inch/cm, use larger needles; to get more stitches to the inch/cm, use smaller needles.

Knitting in the round may tighten the gauge, so if you measured the gauge on a flat swatch, take another gauge reading after you begin your hat. When the hat measures at least 2"/5cm, lay it flat and measure over the stitches in the center of the piece, as the side stitches may be distorted. Keep in mind that if you consciously try to loosen your tension to match the flat knit swatch, you can prevent having to go up a needle size.

YARN SELECTION

For an exact reproduction of the hats photographed, use the yarn listed in the "Materials" section of the pattern. We've chosen yarns that are readily available in the U.S. and Canada at the time of printing. The Resources list on page 175 provides addresses of yarn distributors. Contact them for the name of a retailer in your area. In a few cases, for patterns previously published in *Vogue Knitting,* the original yarns have been discontinued. In those instances, we have provided substitutions and listed the original yarn information on page 174.

Yarn Substitution

You may wish to substitute yarns. Perhaps you view small-scale projects as a chance to incorporate leftovers from your yarn stash, or the yarn specified is not available in your area. You'll need to knit to the given gauge to obtain the knitted measurements with a substitute yarn. Be sure to consider how the fiber content of the substitute yarn will affect the comfort and the ease of care of your hat.

To facilitate yarn substitution, we give a grading number, determined by the stitch gauge obtained in stockinette stitch, in the "Materials" section of the pattern. Look for a substitute yarn that falls into the same category. The suggested gauge on the ball band should also be comparable to that on the Standard Yarn Weight System table on page 175.

After you've successfully gauge-swatched a substitute yarn, you'll need to figure out how much of the substitute yarn the project requires. First, find the total length of the original yarn in the pattern (multiply number of balls by yards/meters per ball). Divide this figure by the new yards/meters per ball (listed on the ball band). Round up to the next whole number to get the required number of balls.

FOLLOWING CHARTS

Charts are a convenient way to follow colorwork, lace, cable, and other stitch patterns at a glance. For our stitch charts, we use the universal knitting language of "symbolcraft." When knitting in the round, read charts from right to left on every round, repeating any stitch and row repeats as directed in the pattern. When knitting back and forth in rows, read charts from right to left on right-side (RS) rows and from left to right on wrong-side (WS) rows. Posting a self-adhesive note under your working row is an easy way to keep your place on a chart.

Blocking

Blocking is an all-important finishing step in the knitting process. Most hats retain their shape after pressing if the blocking stages in the instructions are followed carefully. If you plan to make several hats, invest in a head form. They can be purchased from mail order sources and are made of wood, wire, or Styrofoam. If you don't have a headform, an inverted bowl will make a reasonable substitute.

Wet Block Method

Place the hat on a head form and lightly dampen using a spray bottle. Allow to dry before removing. To achieve a flat crisp edge on tams and berets, wet the knitted piece and insert a dinner plate (of appropriate size). Leave the hat to dry (with the plate in place) on a towel.

Steam Block Method

Using a head form or plate as described, steam lightly using a steam iron or steamer approximately 2"/5cm above the knitting. Do not press or the stitches will become flattened.

SIZING

All of the hats in this book are sized for women. To avoid making a hat that is too tight, or too loose, measure for head size before you begin to knit. Sizing is particularly important for structured hat styles. To measure, place a tape measure across the forehead about ½"/1cm above the ears and measure around the full circumference of the head. Keep the tape snug for accurate results. Note that the circumference of most knitted hats is smaller than the wearer's head itself because these hats stretch.

To determine which size hat to knit, check your head size against the chart below. To change the fit of your hat or cap style, you can experiment with needles sized smaller (for a closer fit) or larger (for a looser fit). Or you may wish to eliminate rows or pattern bands for a shallower hat, or add rows or bands for a deeper hat.

Many of the hats are sized for one size only. In that case, look at the circumference of the finished hat (noted under "Knitted Measurements"). The circumference should be close to your head circumference or smaller, depending on the style. ■

Head Sizes Used in This Book	
X-SMALL	20"/51cm
SMALL	21"/53cm
MEDIUM	22"/56cm
LARGE	23"/59cm

The Patterns

Vogue Knitting The Ultimate Hat Book includes fifty patterns for knitted hats, divided into five chapters. In "Basic Shapes," you'll find one hat that represents each type of hat described on pages 12 and 13. The hat designs aren't necessarily basic, though; they feature a variety of techniques. "Cables," "Lace," and "Color" each explore the use of different stitch patterns in hats. In "Embellishments," the little extras that can take a hat from ho-hum to fabulous take center stage. To cap it all off, at the end of the book we've included helpful information, such as abbreviations, needle sizes, a skill level key, a list of resources for finding the yarns used in the patterns, and more.

BASIC SHAPES

CABLES

LACE

COLOR

EMBELLISHMENTS

Bowler

Wendy Greif's dapper menswear-inspired hat will bowl you over with its functionality and panache. Felting it gives it extra structure.

SIZE

Instructions are written for one size.

KNITTED MEASUREMENTS

Circumference approx 23"/58.5cm

Length approx 9"/23cm

MATERIALS

• 2 3½oz/100g hanks (each approx 109yd/100m) Lopi/Westminster Fibers *Alafoss Lopi* (wool) in #0058 dark grey (MC) (5)

• 1 hank in #9210 burgundy (CC)

• One size 10 (6mm) circular needle, 16"/40cm long, OR SIZE TO OBTAIN GAUGE

• One set (5) size 10 (6mm) double-pointed needles (dpns)

• Stitch marker

GAUGE

13 sts and 21 rnds = 4"/10cm over St st using size 10 (6mm) needle (before felting).

18 sts = 5"/12.5cm and 26 rnds = 4"/10cm over St st using size 10 (6mm) needle (after felting).

TAKE TIME TO CHECK GAUGES.

BOWLER

Brim

With circular needle and MC, cast on 96 sts. Join and pm, taking care not to twist sts on needle.

Next 23 rnds With MC, knit.

Next (dec) rnd *K6, k2tog; rep from * around—84 sts.

Next rnd With MC, knit.

Rise

Next 14 rnds With CC, knit. Cut CC.

Next 12 rnds With MC, knit.

Crown shaping

Change to dpns (dividing sts evenly among 4 needles) when there are too few sts on circular needle. Cont with MC only as foll:

Dec rnd 1 K8, *SKP, k1, k2tog, k16; rep from * around, end last rep k8 (instead of k16)—76 sts.

Next rnd Knit.

Dec rnd 2 K7, *SKP, k1, k2tog, k14; rep from * around, end last rep k7 (instead of k14)—68 sts.

Next rnd Knit.

Dec rnd 3 K6, *SKP, k1, k2tog, k12; rep from * around, end last rep k6 (instead of k12)—60 sts.

Next rnd Knit.

Dec rnd 4 K5, *SKP, k1, k2tog, k10; rep from * around, end last rep k5 (instead of k10)—52 sts.

Next rnd Knit.

Dec rnd 5 K4, *SKP, k1, k2tog, k8; rep from * around, end last rep k4 (instead of k8)—44 sts.

Next rnd Knit.

Dec rnd 6 K3, *SKP, k1, k2tog, k6; rep from * around, end last rep k3 (instead of k6)—36 sts.

Next rnd Knit.

Dec rnd 7 K2, *SKP, k1, k2tog, k4; rep from *

around, end last rep k2 (instead of k4)—28 sts.

Next rnd Knit.

Dec rnd 8 K1, *SKP, k1, k2tog, k2; rep from * around, end last rep k1 (instead of k2)—20 sts.

Next rnd Knit.

Dec rnd 9 *SKP, k1, k2tog; rep from * around—12 sts.

Next rnd Knit.

Dec rnd 10 [K2tog] 6 times—6 sts. Cut MC, leaving an 8"/20.5cm tail, and thread through rem sts. Pull tog tightly and secure end.

FINISHING

Weave in ends.

Felting

To shape hat, you will need a bowl that fits your head. Place hat in washing machine set to hot wash/cold rinse with low water level. Also add a pair of jeans for abrasion and balanced agitation. Add 1 tablespoon dishwashing detergent and ¼ cup baking soda at beginning of wash cycle. Repeat the cycle, if necessary, until piece has shrunk but can be stretched over the bowl. Let hat air dry. Roll up brim to CC stripe, as shown. ■

Pillbox Hat

Nichole Reese's structured pillbox is full of eye-catching design elements, including two geometric stranded color patterns, Latvian braid around the lower edge, and two bands of tuck stitching that frame the crown.

SIZE
Instructions are written for one size.

KNITTED MEASUREMENTS
Brim circumference approx 21½"/54.5cm
Diameter 7¼"/18.5cm
Length 5"/12.5cm

MATERIALS
• 1 1¾oz/50g hank (each approx 144yd/133m) of Berroco *Ultra Alpaca Light* (alpaca/wool) each in #4285 oceanic mix (MC) and #4294 turquoise mix (CC) (3)

• One size 4 (3.5mm) circular needle, 16"/40cm long, OR SIZE TO OBTAIN GAUGE

• One set (5) size 4 (3.5mm) double-pointed needles (dpns)

• Stitch marker

GAUGE
26 sts and 30 rnds = 4/10cm over chart pats using size 4 (3.5mm) needle.
TAKE TIME TO CHECK GAUGE.

NOTE

To work in the rnd, always read charts from right to left.

LATVIAN BRAID

Latvian braid is created by carrying color not in use across RS of work, rather than WS.

Rnd 1 *K1 with MC, k1 with CC; rep from * around.

Rnd 2 Reel off long lengths of both colors. Bring both colors forward to RS. P1 with MC, p1 with CC, matching colors in the round below. Keep colors alternating and always bring the next color to purl over the last stitch. This will twist the yarn as you purl around hat.

Rnd 3 P1 with MC, p1 with CC, matching colors in the round below. Keep colors alternating and always bring the next color to purl under the last stitch. This will release the twist from the yarn as you purl around hat.

Work rnds 1–3 for Latvian braid.

HAT

With circular needle and MC, cast on 140 sts. Join and pm, taking care not to twist sts on needle.

Work rnds 1–3 of Latvian braid. Cont in St st (knit every rnd) and work as foll:

Beg chart 1

Rnd 1 (RS) Work 7-st rep 20 times. Cont to foll chart in this way through rnd 11.

First tuck

Next 6 rnds With CC, knit; leave MC attached, but do not carry yarn up.

Next (tucking) rnd *On WS, use RH needle to pick up the MC purl bump just below the first row of CC color change and place on LH needle, using

MC, k2tog (purl bump and next st on LH needle); rep from * around.

Next rnd With MC, knit.

Beg chart 2

Rnd 1 (RS) Work 7-st rep 20 times. Cont to foll chart in this way through rnd 19.

Next rnd With MC, knit.

Next (dec) rnd *K12, k2tog; rep from * around—130 sts.

Second tuck

Work as for first tuck.

Next (garter ridge) rnd With MC, purl.

Crown shaping

Change to dpns (dividing sts evenly among 4 needles) when there are too few sts on circular needle. Cont to work with MC only as foll:

Rnd 1 (dec) K12, [S2KP, k23] 4 times, S2KP, k11—120 sts.

Rnds 2–3 Knit.

Rnd 4 (dec) K11, [S2KP, k21] 4 times, S2KP, k10—110 sts.

Rnds 5–6 Knit.

Rnd 7 (dec) K10, [S2KP, k19] 4 times, S2KP, k9—100 sts.

Rnds 8 and 9 Knit.

Rnd 10 (dec) K9, [S2KP, k17] 4 times, S2KP, k8—90 sts.

Rnds 11 and 12 Knit.

Rnd 13 (dec) K8, [S2KP, k15] 4 times, S2KP, k7—80 sts.

Rnds 14 and 15 Knit.

Rnd 16 (dec) K7, [S2KP, k13] 4 times, S2KP, k6—70 sts.

Rnd 17 Knit.

Rnd 18 (dec) K6, [S2KP, k11] 4 times, S2KP, k5—60 sts.

Rnd 19 Knit.

Rnd 20 (dec) K5, [S2KP, k9] 4 times, S2KP, k4—50 sts.

Rnd 21 Knit.

Rnd 22 (dec) K4, [S2KP, k7] 4 times, S2KP, k3—40 sts.

Rnd 23 Knit.

Rnd 24 (dec) K3, [S2KP, k5] 4 times, S2KP, k2—30 sts.

Rnd 25 Knit.

Rnd 26 (dec) K2, [S2KP, k3] 4 times, S2KP, k1—20 sts.

Rnd 27 (dec) K1, [S2KP, k1] 4 times, S2KP—10 sts.

Rnd 28 (dec) [K2tog] 5 times—5 sts. Cut MC, leaving an 8"/20.5cm tail, and thread through rem sts. Pull tog tightly and secure end.

FINISHING

Wash and block hat, pinning down bottom edge to prevent it from rolling up. ■

CHART 1

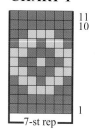

11
10

1

7-st rep

CHART 2

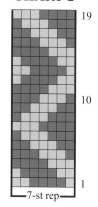

19

10

1

7-st rep

Color Key

■ Oceanic mix (MC)

□ Turquoise mix (CC)

Beanie

Linda Medina's close-fitting topper is inspired by the spiraling lace pattern of a classic Juliet cap. It's stitched in the round in a knit/purl pattern that adds a lot of texture to a basic beanie shape.

SIZE

Instructions are written for one size.

KNITTED MEASUREMENTS

Head circumference 21"/53.5cm

Length 8¼"/21cm

MATERIALS

• 2 1¾/50g balls (each approx 153yd/140m) of Universal Yarn, Inc. *Eden Silk* (wool/silk) in #08 amethyst ⓷

• Size 6 (4mm) circular needle, 16"/40cm long, OR SIZE TO OBTAIN GAUGE

• One set (5) size 6 (4mm) double-pointed needles (dpns)

• Stitch marker

GAUGE

29 sts and 31 rnds = 4"/10cm over stitch pattern using size 6 (4mm) needle.
TAKE TIME TO CHECK GAUGE.

SPIRAL PATTERN

(multiple of 17 sts)

Rnd 1 *Yo, k2 tbl, [p3, k2 tbl] twice, SKP, k3; rep from * around.

Rnd 2 *Yo, p1, [k2 tbl, p3] twice, k1 tbl, SKP, k3; rep from * around.

Rnd 3 *Yo, p2, [k2 tbl, p3] twice, SKP, k3; rep from * around.

Rnd 4 *Yo, [p3, k2 tbl] twice, p2, SKP, k3; rep from * around.

Rnd 5 *Yo, k1 tbl, [p3, k2 tbl] twice, p1, SKP, k3; rep from * around.

Rnd 6 *Yo, k2 tbl, [p3, k2 tbl] twice, SKP, k3; rep from * around.

Rnd 7 *Yo, p1, [k2 tbl, p3] twice, k1 tbl, SKP, k3; rep from * around.

Rep rnds 1–7 for spiral pattern.

BEANIE

Cast on 152 sts. Join, taking care not to twist sts, and place marker for beg of rnd. Slip this marker every rnd.

Work 11 rnds in k1, p1 rib as foll: *k1, p1; rep from * around.

Next (inc) rnd *K1, p1; rep from * to last st, pf&b—153 sts.

Beg spiral pat

Work rnd 1 of spiral pat 9 times around.
Cont to work spiral pat in this manner until rnd 7 is complete. Rep rnds 1–7 four times more.

Crown shaping

Note Change to dpns when there are too few sts to fit comfortably on circular needle.

Rnd 1 (dec) *Yo, [k2 tbl, p3] twice, k2tog tbl, SKP, k3; rep from * around—144 sts.

Rnd 2 (dec) [Yo, p1, k2 tbl, p3, k2 tbl, p1, p2tog, SKP, k3] 9 times around—135 sts.

Rnd 3 (dec) [Yo, p2, k2 tbl, p3, k1 tbl, k2tog tbl, SKP, k3] 9 times around—126 sts.

Rnd 4 (dec) [Yo, p3, k2 tbl, p2, p2tog, SKP, k3] 9 times around—117 sts.

Rnd 5 (dec) [Yo, k1 tbl, p3, k2 tbl, p2tog, SKP, k3] 9 times around—108 sts.

Rnd 6 (dec) [Yo, k2 tbl, p3, k2tog tbl, SKP, k3] 9 times around—99 sts.

Rnd 7 (dec) [Yo, p1, k2 tbl, p1, p2tog, SKP, k3] 9 times around—90 sts.

Rnd 8 (dec) [Yo, k2 tbl, p1, p2tog, SKP, k3] 9 times around—81 sts.

Rnd 9 (dec) [Yo, p1, k1 tbl, p2tog, SKP, k3] 9 times around—72 sts.

Rnd 10 (dec) [Yo, p1, k2tog tbl, SKP, k3] 9 times around—63 sts.

Rnd 11 (dec) [Yo, p2tog, SKP, k3] 9 times around—54 sts.

Rnd 12 (dec) [K1 tbl, p2tog, k3] 9 times around—45 sts.

Rnd 13 (dec) [P2tog, k3] 9 times around—36 sts.

Rnd 14 (dec) [K2tog, k2] 9 times around—27 sts.

Rnd 15 (dec) [K2tog, k1] 9 times around—18 sts.

Rnd 16 (dec) [K2tog] 9 times around—9 sts.

Cut yarn, leaving a long tail. Thread tail through rem sts twice. Draw up and secure. ∎

Watch Cap

Norah Gaughan's snug watch cap is knit in a neutral tweed and subtly embellished with a cable and blossom pattern. It's sure to be your go-to fall hat.

SIZE

Instructions are written for one size.

KNITTED MEASUREMENTS

Circumference (around brim) 17"/43cm
Length (unfolded) 10½"/26.6cm

MATERIALS

• 2 1¾oz/50g balls (each approx 130yd/119m) of Berroco, Inc. *Blackstone Tweed* (wool/super kid mohair/angora) in #2602 steamers (4)

• One pair each sizes 5 and 7 (3.75 and 4.5mm) needles OR SIZE TO OBTAIN GAUGE

• Cable needle (cn)

GAUGE

18 sts and 25 rows = 4"/10cm over St st, using larger needles. TAKE TIME TO CHECK GAUGE.

K2, P2 RIB

Row 1 *K2, p2; rep from * to last 2 sts, k2.
Row 2 K the knit sts, and p the purl sts.
Rep row 2 for k2, p2 rib.

MAKE BOBBLE

K in (front, back, front, back) of same st, [sl 4 sts just made to LH needle, pull yarn tight behind work and k4] twice, pass the last 3 sts, one at a time, over the first st.

STITCH GLOSSARY

3-st RC Sl 1 st to cn and hold to *back*, k2, k1 from cn.
3-st LC Sl 2 sts to cn and hold to *front*, k1, k2 from cn.
4-st RC Sl 2 sts to cn and hold to *back*, k2, k2 from cn.
4-st LC Sl 2 sts to cn and hold to *front*, k2, k2 from cn.
5-st LC Sl 2 sts to cn and hold to *front*, k3, k2 from cn.

NOTE

K1 tbl and p1 tbl are worked into the yo made in the previous row.

CAP

With larger needles, cast on 14 sts.
Purl 1 row on WS.

Beg chart

Next row K1, work chart row 1 four times, k1. Keeping first and last st of every row in St st (k on RS, p on WS), complete the 44 rows of chart—134 sts. Change to smaller needles.
Next (dec) row (RS) In each chart section work as foll: *[k1, k2tog] 3 times, k2; rep from * twice more— 98 sts. Work in k2, p2 rib for 4"/10cm. Bind off.

FINISHING

Sew seam, reversing the RS 3"/7.5cm from lower edge. ■

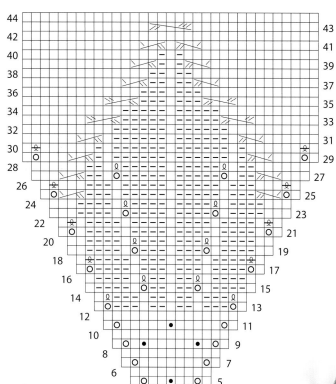

Stitch Key

☐	k on RS, p on WS
⊟	p on RS, k on WS
Ⓞ	yo
●	make bobble
ℚ	k1tbl
⊞	p1tbl
⬲	3-st RC
⬳	3-st LC
⬱	4-st RC
⬰	4-st LC
⬴	5-st LC

Beg chart pat

Rnd 1 Work 24-st rep 7 times. Cont to foll chart in this way through rnd 36.

Crown shaping

Change to dpns (dividing sts evenly among 4 needles) when there are too few sts on circular needle.

Rnd 37 (dec) Work the first S2KP of first rep of chart using the last st from rnd 36 and the first 2 sts of rnd 37, then cont to rep chart 6 times more—154 sts.

Rnds 38 and 39 Work 22-st rep 7 times.

Rnd 40 (dec) Work the first S2KP of first rep of chart using the last st from rnd 39 and the first 2 sts of rnd 40, then cont to rep chart 6 times more—140 sts.

Rnds 41 and 42 Work 20-st rep 7 times.

Rnd 43 (dec) Work the first S2KP of first rep of chart using the last st from rnd 42 and the first 2 sts of rnd 43, then cont to rep chart 6 times more—126 sts.

Rnds 44 and 45 Work 18-st rep 7 times.

Rnd 46 (dec) Work the first S2KP of first rep of chart using the last st from rnd 45 and the first 2 sts of rnd 46, then cont to rep chart 6 times more—112 sts.

Rnds 47 and 48 Work 16-st rep 7 times. Cont to work each dec rnd as established to top of chart. Cut MC, leaving an 8"/20.5cm tail, and thread through rem 14 sts twice. Pull tog tightly and secure end. Cut rem colors and weave in on WS.

FINISHING

To block, wet beret, then gently squeeze out water without wringing. Roll beret in a terry towel to absorb excess moisture. Insert an 11"/28cm dinner plate inside beret. Arrange beret evenly over plate. Invert a wide-bottomed glass on work surface, then place plate on top. Let dry. ■

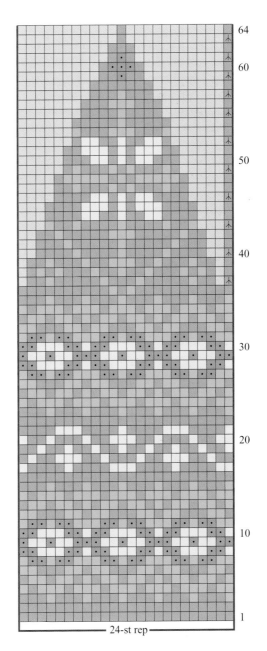

24-st rep

Color Key
- Wensley (MC)
- Richmond (A)
- Hubberholme (B)
- Nappa (C)

Stitch Key
- S2KP
- no stitch

Bucket Hat

This charming hat by Lipp Holmfeld shows that the simple contrast of stockinette stitch and garter stitch can make a strong impression.

SIZE

Instructions are written for one size.

KNITTED MEASUREMENTS

Circumference 18"/45.5cm

MATERIALS

• 2 3½oz/100g hanks (each approx 100yd/91m) of Blue Sky Alpacas *Worsted Hand Dyes* (alpaca/merino wool) in #2015 putty (A) (4)

• 1 hank in #2016 chocolate (B)

• One each size 9 (5.5mm) circular needles, 16"/40cm and 24"/60cm long, OR SIZE TO OBTAIN GAUGE

• One extra size 9 (5.5mm) needle

• 20"/51cm long, ½"/12.5mm wide elastic

• Stitch marker

GAUGES

12 sts and 16 rows = 4"/10cm over garter st with 2 strands of yarn held tog.
16 sts and 20 rows = 4"/10cm over St st with 1 strand of yarn. TAKE TIME TO CHECK GAUGES.

Brim

With 2 strands of A held tog and longer circular needle, cast on 96 sts. Place marker and join for knitting in the round, taking care not to twist sts. [P 1 rnd, k 1 rnd] twice, p 1 rnd.

Dec rnd 1 *K10, k2tog; rep from *around—88 sts. P 1 rnd. **Dec rnd 2** K5, *k2tog, k9; rep from * to last 6 sts, k2tog, k4—80 sts. P 1 rnd, k 1 rnd, p 1 rnd. **Dec rnd 3** *K8, k2tog; rep from * around—72 sts. P 1 rnd, k 1 rnd, p 1 rnd. **Dec rnd 4** K4, *k2tog, k7; rep from * to last 5 sts, k2tog, k3—64 sts. P 1 rnd, k 1 rnd, p 1 rnd. **Dec rnd 5** *K6, k2tog; rep from * around—56 sts. P 1 rnd, k 1 rnd, p 1 rnd. **Dec rnd 6** K3, *k2tog, k5; rep from * to last 4 sts, k2tog, k2—48 sts. P 1 rnd, k 1 rnd, p 1 rnd.

Crown

Change to shorter circular needle and single strand of B, and work in St st as foll: **Next (inc) rnd** *K1, inc 1 st in next st; rep from * around—72 sts. K 4 rnds even. Leave sts on circular needle.

Casing

Turn hat WS facing, with longer circular needle and single strand of B, pick up and k 72 sts at border of brim and crown. **Note** Do not join. This will form slit for elastic. Work 3 rows in St st. With RS facing and shorter circular needle, knit tog 1 st from each needle, closing casing. Work even until crown measures 7"/18cm.

FINISHING

Next rnd Work 36 sts. Turn inside out. Place last 36 sts on extra needle. Bind off all sts using 3-needle bind-off. Turn hat right side out, sew corners of top together.

Thread elastic through casing and adjust to fit. ■

Tuque

English roses and ivy meander around the crown of Sheila Joynes's chic topper. Stitched in the round from the corrugated rib band up, this is a terrific first Fair Isle project for an otherwise experienced knitter.

SIZE

Instructions are written for one size.

KNITTED MEASUREMENTS

Circumference (at brim) 20½"/52cm
Length 11½"/29cm

MATERIALS

• Two 1¾oz/50g skeins (each approx 137yd/125m) of Knit One Crochet Too *Ambrosia* (baby alpaca/silk/cashmere) each in #688 French blue (A) and #633 cornflower (B) (**2**)
[**Note** Yarn used in original pattern is no longer available. Original yarn is listed on page 175.]

• 1 skein each in #249 garnet (C), #591 blue spruce (D), #767 purple heather (E), and #918 fog (F)

• One size 5 (3.75mm) circular needle, 16"/40cm long, OR SIZE TO OBTAIN GAUGE

• One set (5) size 5 (3.75mm) double-pointed needles (dpns)

• Stitch markers

GAUGE

28 sts and 32 rnds (after blocking) = 4"/10cm over chart pat using size 5 (3.75mm) needle. TAKE TIME TO CHECK GAUGE.

TUQUE

With circular needle and A, cast on 140 sts, pm and join, being careful not to twist sts. Work in corrugated rib as foll:
Next 2 rnds P2 A, k2 F.
Next 2 rnds P2 C, k2 F.
Next 2 rnds P2 C, k2 B.
Next 2 rnds P2 D, k2 B.
Next 2 rnds P2 D, k2 E.
Next 2 rnds P2 A, k2 E.
With A, knit 1 rnd.
Next (inc) rnd Cont with A, *k7, M1; rep from * around—160 sts.

Beg chart

Note Place markers every 20 sts.
Rnd 1 Work 20 st pat rep 8 times around.
Cont to work chart, joining and breaking colors as needed, until 60 rows of chart are complete.

Crown shaping

Next rnd With A, knit.
Next (dec) rnd *K2tog, k to 3 sts before next marker, ssk, k1; rep from * around—144 sts. K 2 rnds.
Next rnd With C, knit.

Beg color pat

Rnd 1 *K1 A, k1 B; rep from * around.
Rnd 2 (dec) *With A, k2tog, [k1 A, k1 B] to 4 sts

before marker, k1 B, with A, ssk, k1 B; rep from *
around—128 sts.

Rnd 3 K A sts with B and k B sts with A.

Rnd 4 (dec) *With B, k2tog, [k1 B, k1 A] to 4 sts
before marker, k1 A, with B, ssk, k1 A; rep from *
around—112 sts.

Rnd 5 Rep rnd 3.

Rep rnds 2–5 once more—80 sts. Rep rnd 2, then
rnd 4, then rnd 2 once more—32 sts. Work 1 rnd
even. Cut yarn, leaving long tails.

Thread needle with yarn tails and draw through
rem sts tightly, being careful not to break yarns. ■

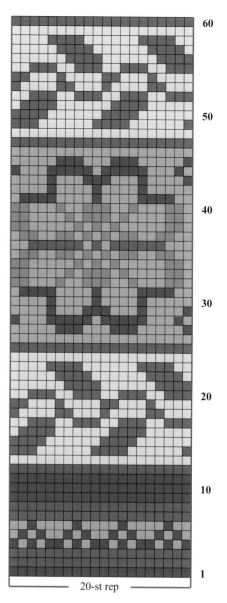

20-st rep

Color Key

■ French blue (A)   ■ Blue spruce (D)
▨ Cornflower (B)   ▨ Purple heather (E)
▨ Garnet (C)   ▢ Fog (F)

Newsboy Cap

Lipp Holmfeld's cap combines a bit of equestrian élan with its newsboy sass. The solid-color cap and visor are livened up with a two-color slip-stitch hound's-tooth-pattern band.

KNITTED MEASUREMENTS

Head circumference approx 21"/53.5cm

MATERIALS

• 1 3½oz/100g skein (each approx 110yd/100m) of Plymouth Yarn Co. *Baby Alpaca Grande* (alpaca) each in #202 camel (A) and #500 black (B) (5)

• One size 10 (6mm) circular needle, 16"/40cm long, OR SIZE TO OBTAIN GAUGE

• One set (5) size 10 (6mm) double-pointed needles (dpns)

• Elastic band ⅜"/10mm wide by 25"/63.5cm long

• Small piece of plastic for inside of visor

• Stitch marker

GAUGE

12 sts and 20 rnds = 4"/10cm over St st using size 10 (6mm) needles.
TAKE TIME TO CHECK GAUGE.

CAP

Inside band

With circular needle and A, cast on 64 sts. Join, taking care not to twist sts on needle. Place marker for end of rnd and sl marker every rnd. K 5 rnds. Remove marker.

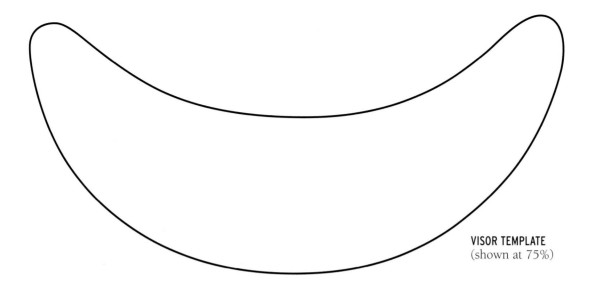

VISOR TEMPLATE
(shown at 75%)

Visor

Next rnd P46, turn work.

Next row P28. Cont in rows over these 28 sts as foll:

Row 1 (RS) SKP, k24, k2tog.

Row 2 P26.

Row 3 SKP, k22, k2tog.

Row 4 P24. Cont in this way to dec 1 st each side until there are 16 sts, end with a RS row.

Next row (WS) K16.

Inc row (RS) K1, M1, work to last st, M1, k1. P 1 row. Rep last 2 rows 5 times more—28 sts.

Next row (RS) P28 on visor, p18 from band. Place marker for center back of band. Cont to work in rnds over all 64 sts as foll: K 2 rnds A, 1 rnd B, 2 rnds A.

Inc rnd With A, [k2, inc 1 in next st] 20 times, [inc 1 in next st] 3 times, k1—87 sts.

Beg hound's-tooth pat

Rnd 1 With B, *sl 1, k2; rep from * around.

Rnd 2 With B, purl.

Rnd 3 With A, *k2, sl 1; rep from * around.

Rnd 4 With A, purl. Rep rnds 1—4 four times more. Rep rnds 1 and 2 once more. Cont with A to end of cap. K next rnd, inc 1 st in center of rnd—88 sts. K 3 rnds.

Top shaping

Next rnd [K9, p2tog] 8 times—80 sts. K 2 rnds even.

Next rnd [K8, p2tog] 8 times—72 sts. K 2 rnds.

Next rnd [K7, p2tog] 8 times—64 sts. K 2 rnds.

Next rnd [K6, p2tog] 8 times—56 sts. K 2 rnds. Change to 4 dpns (14 sts on each needle).

Next rnd [K5, p2tog] 8 times—48 sts. K 2 rnds.

Next rnd [K4, p2tog] 8 times—40 sts. K 2 rnds.

Next rnd [K3, p2tog] 8 times—32 sts.

Next rnd [K2tog] 16 times. Cut yarn and draw through rem 16 sts. Pull tightly to close.

FINISHING

Enlarge template to 100 percent on photocopier. Cut plastic, following template. Sew shaped sides of visor. Insert plastic into visor and sew rem seam of visor to band. Fold band at p row to WS and sew in place, leaving an opening for elastic. Thread elastic through casing, adjust to fit, cut elastic and secure. Stitch closed. ■

Paperbag Hat

Maré Bonnette's charming topper is a cinch. The hat is worked flat with no shaping and seamed, then the crocheted tie is woven through the farrow rib fabric to close the top.

SIZES

Instructions are written for sizes Small (Medium, Large); shown in size Small.

KNITTED MEASUREMENTS

Circumference approx 20 (21¼, 22½)"/51 (54, 57)cm

Length (below tie) approx 7½ (8, 8½)"/19 (20.5, 21.5)cm

MATERIALS

• 2 (3, 3) 1¾oz/50g hanks (each approx 108yd/100m) of Tahki *Cotton Classic* (mercerized cotton) in #3783 bright teal (3)

• One pair size 7 (4.5mm) needles OR SIZE TO OBTAIN GAUGE

• Size H/8 (5mm) crochet hook

GAUGE

21 sts and 30 rows = 4"/10cm over farrow rib using size 7 (4.5mm) needles.
TAKE TIME TO CHECK GAUGE.

FARROW RIB

(over a multiple of 3 sts plus 1)
Row 1 (RS) *K2, p1; rep from *, end k1.
Row 2 P1, *k2, p1; rep from * to end.
Rep rows 1 and 2 for farrow rib.

HAT

Cast on 106 (112, 118) sts. Cont in farrow rib and work even until piece measures 9½ (10, 10½)"/24 (25.5, 26.5)cm from beg, end with a WS row. Bind off in rib.

FINISHING

Sew back seam.

Tie

With crochet hook and 3 strands of yarn held tog, crochet a 24 (25, 26)"/61 (63.5, 66)cm-long chain. Fasten off, leaving a 5"/12.5cm tail for tassel. Measuring 2"/5cm down from bound-off edge, locate and mark center front of hat. Beg and ending 1"/2.5cm on either side of center front, weave chain evenly spaced through fabric 2"/5cm from bound-off edge.

Tassels

Cut 3 strands of yarn 10"/25.5cm long. Thread strands into a large-eye yarn needle. Insert needle through tie, approx ¼"/.5cm from end. Divide strands and tail from chain evenly in half. Tie strands into a firm square knot. Trim strands to 1½"/4cm long. Rep for opposite end of tie. ■

Hood

Jacqueline van Dillen's moss-stitch hood has a scarf built right in, so your neck will stay as warm as your head and your accessories will always be perfectly coordinated.

SIZE

Instructions are written for one size.

KNITTED MEASUREMENTS

Hood approx 12"/30.5cm deep x 11"/28cm high (excluding scarf ends)

Scarf ends approx 12"/30.5cm wide x 27½"/70cm long

MATERIALS

• 8 1¾oz/50g balls (each approx 87yd/80m) of Classic Elite *Ariosa* (extrafine merino) in #4803 foam (5)

• One pair size 10½ (6.5mm) needles OR SIZE TO OBTAIN GAUGE

• Stitch marker

GAUGE

14 sts and 18 rows = 4"/10cm over moss st using size 10½ (6.5mm) needles. TAKE TIME TO CHECK GAUGE.

K1, P1 RIB

(over a multiple of 2 sts plus 1)

Row 1 (RS) K1, *p1, k1; rep from * to end.

Row 2 P1, *k1, p1; rep from * to end.

Rep rows 1 and 2 for k1, p1 rib.

MOSS STITCH

(over a multiple of 2 sts plus 1)

Row 1 (RS) P1, *k1, p1; rep from * to end.

Rows 2 and 3 K1, *p1, k1; rep from * to end.

Row 4 Rep row 1. Rep rows 1–4 for moss st.

HOOD

Cast on 45 sts.

Bottom band

Work in k1, p1 rib for 6 rows, end with a WS row.

Next row (RS) [K1, p1] 3 times (front edge), pm, work row 1 of moss st to end. Keeping 6 sts at front edge in k1, p1 rib as established, cont to work rem sts in moss st. Work even until piece measures approx 76"/193cm from beg, end with row 4 of moss st, dropping marker on last row.

Bottom band

Work in k1, p1 rib for 6 rows. Bind off loosely in rib.

FINISHING

Block piece lightly. Fold piece in half, WS tog and long edges even. Beg at fold, sew back seam for 11"/28cm. ■

Trapper

What could be cozier than a hat knit in bulky wool and alpaca yarn? A brim that covers the back of the neck and wraps around to protect the ears makes Lipp Holmfeld's trapper the ultimate in winter warmth.

SIZE

Instructions are written for one size.

KNITTED MEASUREMENTS

Hat circumference 26"/66cm
From center top to lower edge of brim 10"/25.5cm

MATERIALS

• 3 3½oz/100g balls (each approx 45yd/41m) of Blue Sky Alpacas *Bulky* (wool/alpaca) in #1211 frost (light blue) (6)

• Size 13 (9mm) circular needle, 16"/40cm long, OR SIZE TO OBTAIN GAUGE

• One set (4) size 13 (9mm) double-pointed needles (dpns) OR SIZE TO OBTAIN GAUGE

• Cable needle (cn)

• Size I/9 (5.5mm) crochet hook

• Stitch holder

GAUGES

8 sts and 20 rows = 4"/10cm over garter st using size 13 (9mm) needles.
8 sts and 12 rows = 4"/10cm over cable pat using size 13 (9mm) needles.
TAKE TIME TO CHECK GAUGES.

STITCH GLOSSARY

2-st RC Sl next st to cn and hold in *back*, k1, k1 from cn.
2-st LC Sl next st to cn and hold in *front*, k1, k1 from cn.

TRAPPER

With crochet hook and leaving a 130"/330cm yarn end, ch 26; *starting in 2nd ch from hook, sl st in each ch to end for first tie*; using both yarn ends and long-tail cast-on method, cast on 30 sts for lower edge of back flap; insert crochet hook in last lp on needle and remove it from the needle, ch 26; rep from * to * once more for second tie; place last lp back on needle.

Back flap

Row 1 K30.
Row 2 K, inc 1 st in first and last st of row—32 sts.
Rows 3, 5, 7-12 Knit.
Row 4 Work as for row 2—34 sts.
Row 6 Work as for row 2—36 sts.
Place all sts on holder.

Front flap

Cast on 18 sts.
Work in garter st, inc 1 st at each side every other row 3 times—24 sts. Work 6 rows even in garter

st. Place all 24 sts on circular needle along with 36 sts of back flap—60 sts; k18 sts of back flap, pm for center back, knit 1 rnd to marker.

Crown

Rnds 1, 2, 3, and 4 *P2, k4; rep from * around.

Rnd 5 *P2, 2-st RC, 2-st LC; rep from * around.

Rep rnds 1–5 twice more, work rnds 1–4 once more.

Next rnd *P2tog, 2-st RC, 2-st LC; rep from * around—50 sts.

Next 3 rnds *P1, k4; rep from *around.

Next (dec) rnd *P1, k2tog, SKP; rep from * around—30 sts.

Next 3 rnds *P1, k2; rep from * around.

Next rnd Divide 30 rem sts on 3 dpns (10 sts on each needle), *p1, k2tog; rep from * around—20 sts.

Next rnd *P1, k1; rep from * around.

Last rnd *K2tog; rep from * around—10 sts. Cut yarn, leaving a long end. Draw yarn through all sts and remove from needles. Draw yarn up to close center hole and fasten off. ■

Stocking Cap

Deborah Newton's larger-than-life topper boasts a large flower-and-diamond Fair Isle pattern, wide stripes, and not one, but two fat tassels.

SIZE
Instructions are written for one size.

KNITTED MEASUREMENTS
Head circumference at ribbed band
20"/51cm slightly stretched
Length excluding tassels 28"/71cm

MATERIALS
• 2 1¾oz/50g hanks (each approx 109yd/100m) of Knit One Crochet Too *Brae Tweed* (wool/llama/bamboo/Donegal) in #278 garnet (red A) **4**

• 1 hank each in #525 moss (light green B), #553 moor (light blue C), #682 loch (dark blue D), and #546 olive (dark green E)

• Size 8 (5mm) circular needles, 16"/40cm and 24"/60cm long, OR SIZE TO OBTAIN GAUGE

• Size 6 (4mm) circular needle, 24"/60cm long

• One set (5) size 8 (5mm) double-pointed needles (dpns)

• Cable needle (cn)

• Stitch marker

GAUGE
20 sts and 22 rnds = 4"/10cm over Fair Isle chart pat using larger needles.
TAKE TIME TO CHECK GAUGE.

STITCH GLOSSARY

RT K2tog without slipping sts off LH needle, k next st on LH needle once more, slipping both sts off LH needle tog.

6-st RC Sl 3 sts to cn and hold to *back,* k3, k3 from cn.

CABLE RIB PATTERN

(multiple of 32 sts)

Rnd 1 *K6, [p2, k2] 6 times, p2; rep from * around.

Rnd 2 *6-st RC, [p2, RT, p2, k2] 3 times, p2; rep from * around.

Rnds 3, 5, 7 Rep rnd 1.

Rnds 4, 6, 8 *K6, [p2, RT, p2, k2] 3 times, p2; rep from * around.

Rep rnds 1–8 for cable rib pat.

NOTES

1) Carry color not in use loosely across back, twisting when necessary to avoid long floats.

2) Chart color key indicates symbols for rep 1 and rep 2 of chart. For 3rd rep, use colors for rep 1.

3) Chart is divided into Large Block and 4-st panel for aid in shaping.

CAP

With smaller circular needle, cast on 128 sts. Join, being careful not to twist sts, and pm for beg of rnd. Work in cable rib pat until piece measures 6"/15cm from beg, end with a rnd 4. Dec 17 sts evenly across last rnd—111 sts.

Crown

With B, knit 1 rnd. With E, k 1 rnd, p 1 rnd. Change to larger circular needle.

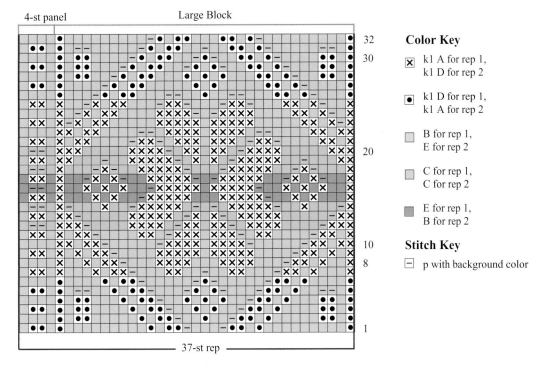

4-st panel   Large Block

Color Key

☒ k1 A for rep 1,
   k1 D for rep 2

⊡ k1 D for rep 1,
   k1 A for rep 2

☐ B for rep 1,
   E for rep 2

☐ C for rep 1,
   C for rep 2

▨ E for rep 1,
   B for rep 2

Stitch Key

⊟ p with background color

32
30

20

10
8

1

— 37-st rep —

Beg chart

Next rnd With colors for rep 1, work rnd 1 of chart 3 times around.

Cont to work chart in this manner until rnd 32 is complete.

Next rnd With colors for rep 2, work rnd 1 of chart 3 times around.

Cont to work chart in this manner until rnd 8 of rep 2 is complete.

Beg shaping

Next (dec) rnd [Ssk in color of first st of Large Block, work to last 2 sts of Large Block, k2tog in color of last st of Large Block, work 4-st panel] 3 times—105 sts.

Work even in chart pat as established, rep dec rnd every 8th rnd 6 times more—69 sts. AT SAME TIME, when rnd 32 of rep 2 is complete, work in colors for rep 1. Cont to work chart and shaping in this manner until rnd 32 of 3rd rep is complete.

Beg stripes

Next (dec) rnd With A, knit, dec 6 sts evenly around—63 sts.

Knit 7 rnds more.

Rep last 8 rnds in colors as foll: E, C, A, D—39 sts.

Next rnd Cont with D, [k1, k2tog] 13 times around—26 sts. Cut yarn, thread through rem sts twice, and tighten.

FINISHING

Weave in all ends. Steam lightly above ribbed section. Do not steam ribbing. Fold ribbed section in half to inside and sew loosely in place.

Long (short) cord (make one of each)

With larger needle and A, cast on 25 (15) sts. Knit 1 row. Bind off knitwise.

Make one 4"/10cm tassel in each of D and E. Tie to cords and sew to top of cap. ∎

Chullo

Bicolored pompoms punctuate the earflaps and point of
Kristin Nicholas's Peruvian hat, which features a garter ridge band,
Fair Isle patterning, and embroidered details.

SIZE

Instructions are written for one size.

KNITTED MEASUREMENTS

Circumference 20"/51cm
Length (from tip, without pompom, to brim)
12"/30.5cm

MATERIALS

• 1 1¾oz/50g skein each (each approx 93yd/85m)
of Classic Elite Yarns *Color by Kristin* (4)
(wool/alpaca/mohair) in #3258 geranium (A),
#3243 yarrow (B), #3281 lichen (C),
#3228 aubergine (D), #3285 pumpkin (E),
#3289 Julia's pink (F), and #3212 deep forest (G)

Note Yarn used in original pattern is no longer
available. Original yarn is listed on page 175.

• One each sizes 5 and 7 (3.75mm and 4.5mm)
circular needles, 16"/40cm long

• One set (5) size 7 (4.5mm) double-pointed
needles (dpns) OR SIZE TO OBTAIN GAUGE

• Tapestry needle and stitch markers

GAUGE

20 sts and 22 rnds = 4"/10cm over chart
patterns, using larger needles.
TAKE TIME TO CHECK GAUGE.

GARTER RIDGE

(over any number of sts in the rnd)
Rnd 1 Knit.
Rnd 2 Purl.
Rnds 1 and 2 make one garter ridge.

NOTE

When working in two-color rounds, take care to
carry the yarn not in use loosely behind work.

CHULLO

With smaller circular needle and A, cast on 90 sts.
Join and place marker (pm) for beg of rnd, being
careful not to twist. Purl one round to complete a
garter ridge. Work 4 more garter ridges in the foll
order: C, D, B, F. Change to larger circular needle,
switching to dpns when there are too few sts to fit
comfortably on needle.

Beg charts
Next (inc) rnd With A, [k9, M1] 10 times—100 sts.
Work chart 1 over next 12 rnds.
Next 2 rnds With C, work one garter ridge.
Next (dec) rnd With D, [k8, k2tog] 10 times—90 sts.
Work chart 2 over next 8 rnds.
Next (dec) rnd With B, [k4, k2tog] 15 times—75 sts.
Purl one rnd. Change to F and G and work chart 3
over next 7 rnds.
Next (dec) rnd With D, *k1, k2tog; rep from *
around—50 sts. Purl one rnd. Change to C and A

and work chart 4 over next 8 rnds.

Next (dec) rnd With G, *k2tog, k1, k2tog; rep from * around—30 sts. Purl one rnd. Change to D and B and work chart 5 over next 6 rnds.

Next (dec) rnd With A, *k1, k2tog; rep from * around—20 sts. Purl one rnd. Change to F and G and work chart 6 over next 4 rnds.

Next (dec) rnd With B, *k2tog; rep from * around— 10 sts. Purl one rnd. Change to D and work in St st (k every rnd) for 6 rnds.

Next (dec) rnd *K2tog, rep from * around—5 sts. Cut yarn and pull through sts to close tip of hat.

Earflaps

With smaller needle and E, cast on 33 sts. Work back and forth as foll:

Row 1 (WS) K16, pm, p1, pm, k16.

Row 2 With D, k14, k2tog, sm, k1, sm, k2tog, k14—31 sts.

Row 3 K15, sm, p1, sm, k15.

Row 4 With C, k13, k2tog, k1, k2tog, k13—29 sts.

Row 5 K14, sm, p1, sm, k14.

Row 6 With E, k10, [k2tog] twice, sm, k1, sm, [k2tog] twice, k10—25 sts.

Row 7 K10, k2tog, sm, p1, sm, k2tog, k10—23 sts.

Row 8 With D, k7, [k2tog] twice, sm, k1, sm, [k2tog] twice, k7—19 sts.

Row 9 K7, k2tog, sm, p1, sm, k2tog, k7—17 sts.

Row 10 With C, k4, [k2tog] twice, sm, k1, sm, [k2tog] twice, k4—13 sts.

Row 11 K4, k2tog, sm, p1, sm, k2tog, k4.

Row 12 With E, k1, [k2tog] twice, sm, k1, sm, [k2tog] twice, k1—7 sts.

Row 13 K1, k2tog, sm, p1, sm, k2tog, k1—5 sts.

Row 14 K2tog, sm, k1, sm, k2tog—3 sts.

Row 15 Bind off rem 3 sts knitwise.

FINISHING

Sew an earflap to each side of chullo.

Embroidery

With D, work the center stitch of each chart 1 motif in duplicate stitch. With 2 strands of C, work a French knot in the center of each diamond on chart 2.

Pompoms

With A and B, make 2 small pompoms and attach to bottoms of earflaps. With A, C, D, and E, make 1 large pompom and attach to top of chullo. ■

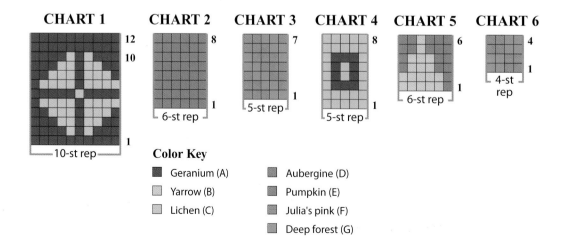

CHART 1   **CHART 2**   **CHART 3**   **CHART 4**   **CHART 5**   **CHART 6**

10-st rep   6-st rep   5-st rep   5-st rep   6-st rep   4-st rep

Color Key

- Geranium (A)
- Yarrow (B)
- Lichen (C)
- Aubergine (D)
- Pumpkin (E)
- Julia's pink (F)
- Deep forest (G)

Cloche

You'll feel like you're stepping into a costume drama when you don Linda Medina's demure cloche with a knit-in band and bow.

SIZES

Instructions are written for size Small/Medium (Large/X-Large); shown in size Large/X-Large.

KNITTED MEASUREMENTS

Crown circumference at band approx
26 (28)"/66 (71)cm
Length to top of brim approx
7½ (8½)"/19 (21.5)cm

MATERIALS

• 1 (1) 1¾oz/50g hank each (each approx 128yds/117m) of Louisa Harding/KFI *Willow Tweed* (alpaca/wool/silk) in #4 ash (A), #5 stone (B), and #16 blush (C) **3**

• Size 5 (3.75mm) circular needle, 16"/40.5cm long, OR SIZE TO OBTAIN GAUGES

• Size 5 (3.75mm) double-pointed needles (dpns)

• 3 removable stitch markers

• Stitch markers

• 2 yarn needles

• Sewing needle and thread to match A

GAUGES

24 sts and 32 rnds to 4"/10cm over pattern st (unstretched).
22 sts and 28 rows to 4"/10cm over St st.
20 sts and 40 rows to 4"/10cm over seed st.
TAKE TIME TO CHECK GAUGES.

STITCH GLOSSARY

Kfb Knit into front and back of next st—1 st increased.
Pfb Purl into front and back of next st—1 st increased.

PATTERN STITCH

(multiple of 4 sts; worked in rows)
Note Do not cut yarn between rows.
Row 1 (RS) With A, *k2, p2; rep from * to end.
Row 2 With A, *k2, p2; rep from * to end
Row 3 With B, purl.

Row 4 With B, knit.

Rows 5 and 6 With A, *k2, p2; rep from * to end.

Row 7 With B, knit.

Row 8 With B, purl.

PATTERN STITCH

(multiple of 4 sts; worked in the rnd)

Note Do not cut yarn between rnds.

Rnds 1, 2, 5, and 6 With A, *p2, k2;
rep from * around.

Rnds 3 and 4 With B, purl.

Rnds 7 and 8 With B, knit.

Rep rnds 1–8 for pattern st.

SEED STITCH

(over an odd number of sts; worked in rows)

Row 1 K1, *p1, k1; rep from * to end.

Rep row 1 for seed st.

CLOCHE

Brim facing

With circular needle and A, cast on 75 sts.
Do not join.

Row 1 (RS) Knit.

Row 2 Purl.

Row 3 K2tog, k to last 2 sts, k2tog—73 sts.

Rep last 2 rows 3 times more — 67 sts.

Purl 1 row on WS. Bind off.

Brim

With circular needle and A, cast on 72 sts.
Do not join.

Beg pattern st in rows

Note Work increases into pattern.

Next row (RS) Work row 1 of pat st in rows.

Next (inc) row Kfb in first st, work row 2 to last st,
kfb—74 sts.

Next row Work row 3 of pat.

Next (inc) row Kfb in first st, work row 4 to last st,
kfb—76 sts.

Next row Work row 5 of pat.

Next (inc) row Kfb in first st, work row 6 to last st,
kfb—78 sts.

Next (inc) row Kfb in first st, work row 7 to last st,
kfb—80 sts.

Next (inc) row Kfb in first st, work row 8 to last st,
kfb—82 sts.

Next (inc) row Kfb in first st, work row 1 over first 6
sts, place a removable marker on last st worked,
cont row 1 to last st, kfb—84 sts. Do not turn
work, cast on 60 (84) sts—144 (168) sts. Be
careful not to twist sts, pm, and join to work in
rnd. Slip the marker at the end of each round.

Crown

Next 2 rnds With B, knit.

Beg pattern st

Note The seed st band will be placed over
these rows later.

Work rnds 1–4 of pattern st.

Rnd 5 With A, [p2,k2, p2, k2tog] around—126
(147) sts.

Rnd 6 [P2, k2, p2, k1] around.

Size S/M only

Rnd 7 With B, knit.

Rnd 8 [K19, k2tog] around—120 sts.

Size L/XL only

Rnd 7 With B, [K4, k2tog] around to last 3 sts, k3—123 sts.

Rnd 8 [K39, k2tog] around—120 sts.

Both sizes

Work rnds 1–8 of pattern st 3 (4) times.

Shape crown

Note Change to dpns when there are too few sts to work comfortably with circular needle.

Next (dec) rnd With A, *[p2, k2] 4 times, p2tog, k2tog; rep from * around—108 sts.

Next (dec) rnd [P2, k2] 3 times, p2, k1, k2tog, p2tog, p1, k2, *[p2, k2] twice, p2, k1, k2tog, p2tog, p1, k2; rep from * 3 times more, [p2, k2] twice, p2, k1, k2tog, move marker 1 st to the left, p2tog—96 sts.

Next 2 rnds With B, purl.

Next 2 rnds With A, p1, *k2, p2; rep from * to last 3 sts, k2, p1.

Next 2 rnds With B, knit.

Next (dec) rnd Move marker 1 st to the left. With A, *[k2, p2] twice, k2tog, p2tog; rep from * around—80 sts.

Next (dec) rnd K2, *p2, k2, p1, p2tog, k2tog, k1; rep from * 6 times more, p2, k2, p1, p2tog, move marker 1 st to the left, k2tog—64 sts.

Next 2 rnds With B, purl.

Next 2 rnds With A, k1, *p2, k2; repeat from * to last 3 sts, p2, k1.

Next 2 rnds With B, knit.

Next (dec) rnd Move marker 1 st to the left. With A, sl first st, *p2tog, k2tog; rep from * around—32 sts.

Next rnd *P2, k2; repeat from * around.

Next 2 rnds With B, purl.

Next 2 rnds With A, *p2, k2; repeat from * around.

Next 2 rnds With B, knit.

Next (dec) rnd With A, *p2tog, k2tog; repeat from * around—16 sts.

Next rnd *P2, k2; repeat from * around.

Next rnd With B, purl. Cut yarns and thread B into a yarn needle. Pull B through rem sts snugly to close. Fasten off.

Seed st band

With C and 2 dpns, cast on 7 sts.

Work in seed st until band fits around entire lower edge of cloche above brim, plus 9"/23cm—approx 35 (37)"/89 (94)cm long. Bind off. Place one removable st marker at 3"/8cm from cast-on edge and a second at 6"/15cm from bound-off edge. With a yarn needle and C, work a line of small running sts along one long side edge of the seed st band; this will be the top edge. Cut C, leaving a short tail.

Seed st loops (make 2)

With C and 2 dpns, cast on 7 sts. Work in seed st until piece measures 7"/18cm. Bind off. Fold each loop in half, pin the ends tog. With C and yarn needle, beg at joined ends and sew 1½"/4cm closed along one side of each loop. Set aside.

FINISHING

With WS facing tog, pin brim facing to brim, stretching brim slightly if necessary. With A and yarn needle, whipstitch closed all around.

Note Read thoroughly before beginning to sew. Match second band marker to brim marker (leaving 6"/15cm tail free), pin band across top of

brim along facing seam, then pin the lower edge of band all along the cast-on edge of crown, end by matching first marker on band to brim marker, leaving 3"/8cm tail free. With a second yarn needle and C, neatly whipstitch lower edge of band to cast-on edge of crown and along top of brim. Place the unsewn edges of folded loops side by side on RS of cloche at brim marker. Seams are facing up. Overlap ends of loops slightly and pin in place. Place 6"/15cm tail over ends of both loops, pin in place. Fold 6"/15cm end to make third loop in same manner and sew inner side edge closed for 1"/2.5cm. Check positioning of all three loops. When you are satisfied with the placement, unpin the third loop, then with C and yarn needle, stitch the ends of the first 2 loops in place. Stitch

third loop in place so that band will hide ends of other loops. Stitch closed any unsewn length along lower edge. Gently pull running st tail to gather top edge of band, fitting it snugly around cloche, leaving 3"/8cm tail free. Pin in place, then whipstitch as before. Pull the running st tail a little more to curve the last 3"/8cm. Pin this end over band and loops, then whipstitch in place, leaving last ½"/1cm free. Remove markers. With a sewing needle and a double strand of sewing thread, tack the top edges of the loops in place, securing to cloche. ■

Cabled Tam

Jennifer Hagen's slouchy tam is worked in the round from the top down, starting on double-pointed needles and changing to circulars. The rich cable pattern and golden beige yarn give it a regal aura.

SIZES

Instructions are written for sizes Small (Medium, Large); shown in size Small.

KNITTED MEASUREMENTS

Brim 19 (21, 23)"/48 (53.5, 58.5)cm
Widest diameter when blocked 12"/30.5cm

MATERIALS

• 5 (5, 5) 1¾oz/50g balls (each approx 87yd/80m) of Filatura di Crosa/Tahki•Stacy Charles, Inc. *Zara 8* (merino) in #1451 oatmeal (4)

Note Yarn used in original pattern is no longer available. Original yarn is listed on page 175.

• One set (6) size 6 (4mm) double-pointed needles (dpns) OR SIZE TO OBTAIN GAUGES

• Size 6 (4mm) circular needle, 24"/60cm long

• Size 5 (3.75mm) circular needle, 16"/40cm long

• Cable needle

• Stitch markers

GAUGES

27 sts and 35 rnds = 4"/10cm over chart 1 using size 6 (4mm) needles.

24 sts and 36 rnds = 4"/10cm over chart 2 using size 5 (3.75mm) needles.
TAKE TIME TO CHECK GAUGES.

STITCH GLOSSARY

3-st RPC Sl 1 st to cn and hold to back, k2, p1 from cn.
3-st LPC Sl 2 sts to cn and hold to front, p1, k2 from cn.
4-st RC Sl 2 sts to cn and hold to back, k2, k2 from cn.
Inc Knit into front and back of stitch.

NOTE

Changes for sizes Medium and Large do not begin until decreasing for brim.

TAM

Cast on 5 sts to one size 6 (4mm) dpn. Inc into each stitch, dividing among 5 dpns (2 sts on each needle). Place marker for end of rnd and join, taking care not to twist sts.
Next rnd Inc into each st—20 sts. Work rnds 1–22 of chart 1, repeating it five times around—240 sts. Change to circular needles when sts no longer fit on dpns and pm for beg of reps.
Note On rnds 31, 35, 39, 43, and 51, only half the cable is shown at beg and end of rep. Cont chart through rnd 51. Change to smaller needle.

CHART 1

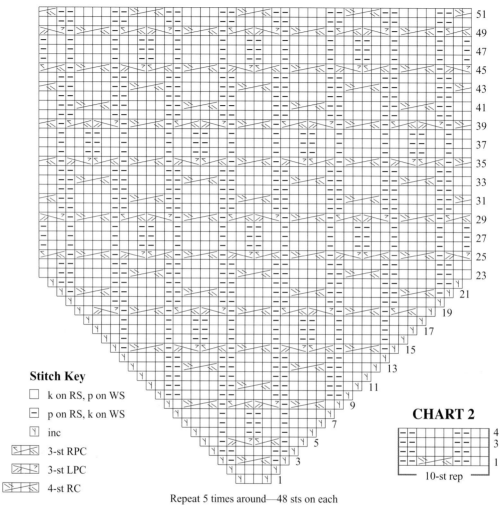

Stitch Key

- ☐ k on RS, p on WS
- ⊟ p on RS, k on WS
- ꓨ inc
- 3-st RPC
- 3-st LPC
- 4-st RC

Repeat 5 times around—48 sts on each
needle when increases are complete.

CHART 2

10-st rep

Brim

Next (dec) rnd (for sizes Small and Medium) *K2tog; rep from * around—120 sts.

Next (dec) rnd (for size Large only) *K1, [k2tog] 6 times; rep from * to last 6 sts, [k2tog, k1] twice—130 sts.

Work rnd 1 of chart 2 as foll:

For size Small only Work first 2 sts of first 5 reps as k2tog, work 10-st rep over next 10 sts, work first 2 sts of last 5 reps as k2tog—110 sts.

For sizes Medium and Large only Work even in chart over 120 (130) sts.

For all sizes Work even in chart 2 until 4 rows have been worked 3 times. Bind off all sts loosely in pat.

FINISHING

Weave in ends. Block on a large dinner plate with the widest part of the hat around the plate rim, pulling the brim in toward the center to prevent its being stretched. ■

Cabled Helmet

Deborah Newton works the oval cables that form the earflaps in a single strip with the cabled band. From there, stitches for the crown are picked up, worked in a trio of separate panels, then sewn together.

SIZE
Instructions are written for one size.

KNITTED MEASUREMENTS
Finished hat at horizontal edge approx 21"/53.5cm (slightly stretched)

MATERIALS
• 2 3½oz/100g hanks (each approx 145yd/136m) of Alpaca With a Twist *Highlander* (alpaca/wool/microfiber/viscose) in #3015 hebrides rose (4)

• One pair size 8 (5mm) needles OR SIZE TO OBTAIN GAUGE

• Cable needle (cn)

• One 1"/25mm button

GAUGE
18 sts and 26 rows = 4"/10cm over St st using size 8 (5mm) needles.
TAKE TIME TO CHECK GAUGE.

STITCH GLOSSARY
3-st RPC Sl 1 st to cn and hold to *back*, k2, p1 from cn.
3-ST LPC Sl 2 sts to cn and hold to *front*, p1, k2 from cn.
4-ST RC Sl 2 sts to cn and hold to *back*, k2, k2 from cn.

4-st LC Sl 2 sts to cn and hold to *front*, k2, k2 from cn.

4-st RPC Sl 2 sts to cn and hold to *back*, k2, p2 from cn.

4-st LPC Sl 2 sts to cn and hold to *front*, p2, k2 from cn.

TWIST CABLE PATTERN

(multiple of 8 sts plus 2)

Rows 1 and 3 (WS) K2, *p6, k2; rep from *.

Row 2 P2, *[k 2nd st in front of first st, then k first st—RT] 3 times, p2; rep from *.

Row 4 P2, *k1, [RT] twice, k1, p2; rep from *.

Rep rows 1–4 for twist cable pat.

LOWER BAND

Right earflap

Cast on 10 sts.

Beg oval chart

Preparation row (WS) K3, p4, K3. Cont in chart pat as established through row 33—10 sts.

Strip for back of hat

Work in twist cable pat until strip measures 4"/10cm, end with a RS row.

Left earflap

Beg on WS with prep row of chart pat, and work through row 33.

Strip for front of hat

Work in twist cable pat until strip measures 5"/12.5cm, end with a row 1 of pat.

Decrease for decorative tip

Next row (RS) P2, [k2tog] 3 times, p2—7 sts.

Next row K2, p3, p2.

Next row P1, k2tog, k3tog, p1—4 sts.

Next row K1, p2, k1.

Cut yarn and pull through rem sts, weave in end. Join the cast-on edge to WS of opposite end at beg of tip shaping and sew ends tog.

Lower edge trim

With RS facing, beg at right earflap, pick up and k 27 sts evenly along cabled right earflap, 22 sts along front strip, 27 sts along left flap, and 19 sts along back strip to end—95 sts. K next row on WS. K next row, inc 5 sts evenly along each earflap section—105 sts. Bind off knitwise on WS. Sew side edge seam.

TOP OF HAT

Center piece

With RS facing, beg at base of join at front, behind tip, pick up and k 40 sts evenly along strip at front.

Next row (WS) P3 (St st edge sts), work row 1 of twisted rib to last 3 sts, p3 (St st edge sts).

Work twist cable pat between 3 edge sts, until center piece measures 12"/30.5cm, end with a pat row 4.

Next row (WS) P3, k2tog, [p6, k2tog] 4 times, end p3—35 sts.

Next row K3, p1, *[k2tog] 3 times, p1; rep from * 3 times more, end k3—23 sts.

Next row P3, k1, *p1, k1; rep from * to last 3 sts, end p3. Bind off.

Sew bound-off edge to top of back strip.

Side piece

With RS of one earflap facing, pick up 32 sts evenly along top edge of the earflap.

Beg textured rib pat

Row 1 (WS) P1 (St st edge st), k2, *p2, k2; rep from *, end p1 (St st edge st).

Row 2 K1, p2, *k2tog tbl but do not drop from needle, knit same 2 sts tog through front loops, drop sts from needle; p2; rep from *, end k1.

Row 3 P1, k2, *p1, yo, p1, k2; rep from *, end p1.

Row 4 K1, p2, *ssk, k1, p2; rep from *, end k1.

Rep rows 1–4 until 4 row reps of pat are complete.

Next row P1, work to last st, p1.

Next (dec) row (RS) Ssk, work to last 2 sts, k2tog—30 sts.

Rep last 2 rows until there are 22 sts. Bind off. Sew sides and bound-off sts of this piece to sides of center piece.

Work in same way along other earflap.

FINISHING

Weave in ends. Sew button at base of shaped tip on front of hat as decorative trim. ■

OVAL CABLE

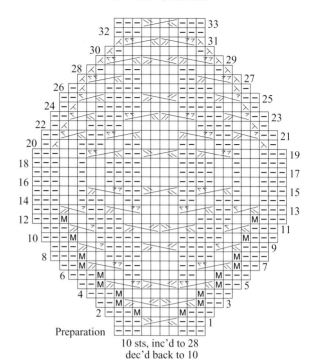

10 sts, inc'd to 28
dec'd back to 10

Stitch Key

☐ k on RS, p on WS

⊟ p on RS, k on WS

Ⓜ M1

k2tog on RS, ssk on WS

ssk on RS, k2tog on WS

3-st RPC

3-st LPC

4-st RC

4-st LC

4-st RPC

4-st LPC

Brimmed Pompom Hat

Devin Cole's funky cap is knit in three pieces—the body, the cuff, and the visor—which are then stitched together. A perky pompom tops it off!

SIZE

Instructions are written for one size.

KNITTED MEASUREMENTS

Circumference (inside) approx 21"/53.5cm

Length (excluding pompom) approx 8"/20.5cm

MATERIALS

• 4 1¾oz/50g balls (each approx 55yd/50m) of Rowan/Westminster Fibers *Felted Tweed Chunky* (superwash merino wool/silk/nylon) in #285 seaweed (6)

• One size 11 (8mm) circular needle, 16"/40cm long, OR SIZE TO OBTAIN GAUGE

• One pair size 11 (8mm) needles

• One set (5) size 11 (8mm) double-pointed needles (dpns)

• Stitch marker

GAUGE

11 sts and 16 rnds = 4"/10cm over St st using size 11 (8mm) needle. TAKE TIME TO CHECK GAUGE.

STITCH GLOSSARY

4-st LC Sl 2 sts to cn and hold to front, k2, k2 from cn.

CABLE RIB STITCH

(over a multiple of 10 sts plus 3)

Rnds 1–4 (RS) *P1, k4, p1, k1, p2, k1; rep from * around, end p2, k1. **Rnd 5** *P1, 4-st LC, p1, k1, p2, k1; rep from * around, end p2, k1. **Rnd 6** Rep rnd 1. Rep rnds 1–6 for cable rib st.

HERRINGBONE STITCH

(over a multiple of 2 sts plus 1)

Row 1 (RS) *K2tog tbl, leaving sts on LH needle, sl first st off LH needle, leaving 2nd st on needle; rep from * to last st, end k1 tbl,. **Row 2** *P2tog tbl, leaving sts on LH needle, sl first st off LH needle, leaving 2nd st on needle; rep from * to last st, end p1 tbl. Rep rows 1 and 2 for herringbone st.

BODY

With straight needles, cast on 26 sts. Knit next row. Beg with a purl row, cont in St st (knit on RS, purl on WS) and work as foll:

Bottom edge shaping

Cast on 5 sts at beg of next 2 rows, 4 sts at beg of next 2 rows, 3 sts at beg of next 2 rows, then 2 sts at beg of next 2 rows. Change to circular needle and cont to work back and forth, cast on 1 st at beg of next 2 rows—56 sts. Join and pm for beg of rnds. Place yarn marker at join for center bottom edge of hat. Work around in St st (knit every rnd) for 11 rnds.

Crown shaping

Change to dpns (dividing sts evenly among 4 needles) when there are too few sts on circular needle.

Dec rnd 1 [K2tog, k6] 7 times—49 sts.

Next 2 rnds Knit.

Dec rnd 2 [K2tog, k5] 7 times—42 sts.

Next 2 rnds Knit.

Dec rnd 3 [K2tog, k4] 7 times—35 sts.

Next rnd Knit.

Dec rnd 4 [K2tog, k3] 7 times—28 sts.

Next rnd Knit.

Dec rnd 5 [K2tog, k2] 7 times—21 sts.

Next rnd Knit. Cut yarn, leaving an 8"/20.5cm tail, and thread through rem sts. Pull tog tightly and secure end.

CUFF

With circular needle, cast on 93 sts. Join and pm, taking care not to twist sts on needle. Rep rnds 1–6 of cable rib pat twice, then rep rnd 1. Bind off in cable rib pat.

VISOR

With straight needles, cast on 29 sts.

Outer edge shaping

Row 1 (RS) Work row 1 of herringbone st. Working new sts into herringbone st, cont to work as foll:

Rows 2-5 Cast on 2 sts, work in herringbone st to end—37 sts.

Rows 6 and 7 Cast on 1 st, work in herringbone st to end—39 sts.

Rows 8-10 Work even in herringbone st.

Inner edge shaping

Cont herringbone st with row 1, work as foll:

Row 1 (RS) Work first 11 sts, place these sts on holder, bind off center 17 sts, work last 11 sts.

Row 2 Work even.

Row 3 Bind off first 3 sts, work to end—8 sts.

Row 4 Work even.

Row 5 Bind off first 3 sts, work to end—5 sts.

Row 6 Work even.

Row 7 Bind off first st, work to end—4 sts.

Row 8 Work even.

Row 9 Bind off first 2 sts, work to end—2 sts.

Row 10 Work even. Bind off. Place 11 sts on holder on LH needle ready for a WS row. Join yarn. For opposite inner edge shaping, rep rows 3–10—2 sts. Bind off.

FINISHING

Steam visor flat; let dry. Fold visor in half, then pin bottom edges only to blocking board. Steam again to create a gentle curve along inner edge; let dry. Mark center bound-off edge on inner edge of visor. Center visor on center bottom edge of hat. Whipstitch visor in place. Place cuff around hat and whipstitch cast-on edge to bottom edge of hat and over sts between visor and hat.

Pompom

Make a 3½"/9cm pompom and sew to top of hat. ■

Bavarian Beanie

Lois S. Young was inspired by Bavarian knitting to create this hat, which borrows its stitch patterns from folk stockings.

SIZE

Instructions are written for one size.

KNITTED MEASUREMENTS

Circumference approx 23"/58.5cm

Length approx 8"/20.5cm

MATERIALS

• 1 3½oz/100g hank (each approx 220yd/201m) Universal *Deluxe Worsted* (wool) in #111835 purple (**4**)

• One size 7 (4.5mm) circular needle, 16"/40cm long, OR SIZE TO OBTAIN GAUGE

• One set (5) size 7 (4.5mm) double-pointed needles (dpns)

• Cable needle (cn)

• Stitch marker

GAUGE

26 sts and 25 rnds = 4"/10cm over chart pat using size 7 (4.5mm) needle (after blocking). TAKE TIME TO CHECK GAUGE.

NOTE

To work in the rnd, always read chart from right to left.

STITCH GLOSSARY

3-st CLC Sl 2 sts to cn and hold to *front*, k1 tbl, return sts from cn to LH needle, sl 1 st to cn and hold to *front,* k1 tbl, k1 tbl from cn.

2-st RC Sl 1 st to cn and hold to *back*, k1 tbl, k1 tbl from cn.

2-st LC Sl 1 st to cn and hold to *front*, k1 tbl, k1 tbl from cn.

2-st RPC Sl 1 st to cn and hold to *back*, k1 tbl, p1 from cn.

2-st LPC Sl 1 st to cn and hold to *front*, p1, k1 tbl from cn.

BEANIE

With circular needle, cast on 148 sts. Join and pm, taking care not to twist sts on needle.

Beg chart pat

Rnd 1 (RS) Work 37-st rep 4 times. Cont to foll chart in this way to rnd 51, changing to dpns (dividing sts evenly among 4 needles) when there are too few sts on circular needle. When rnd 51 is completed, cut yarn, leaving an 8"/20.5 tail, and thread through rem sts twice. Pull tog tightly and secure end.

FINISHING

To block, wet hat, then gently squeeze out water without wringing. Roll hat in a terry towel to absorb excess moisture. Invert a 6"/15cm diameter mixing bowl over a large water glass. Drape hat over bowl, stretching it to conform to curve of bowl; let dry. ■

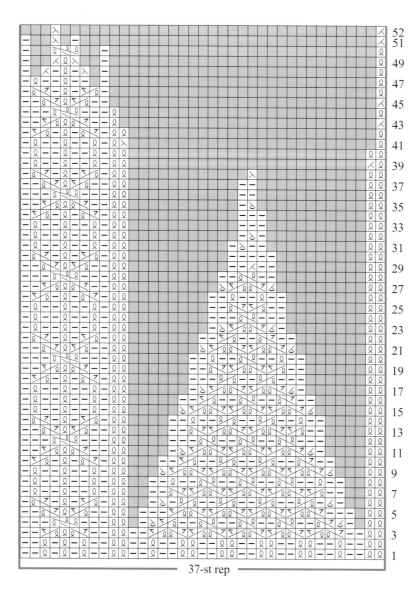

37-st rep

Stitch Key

Ω	k1tbl
−	p
▢	no stitch
⟋	k2tog
⟍	ssk
⟋	p2tog
⟍	p2tog tbl
Ω Ω Ω	3-st CLC
Ω Ω	2-st RC
Ω Ω	2-st LC
Ω −	RPC
− Ω	LPC

Cabled Rib Hood

Little Red Riding Hood never looked as chic as you will in Kathy Perry's playful cabled hood. Picot edging and pompoms on the ties and peak add to the whimsy.

SIZE
Instructions are written for one size.

KNITTED MEASUREMENTS
Approx 9"/23cm deep x 10"/25.5cm high (excluding pom poms and ties)

MATERIALS
• 2 1¾oz/50g balls (each approx 98yd/90m) Bergère de France *Origin Alpaga* (merino wool/baby alpaca) in immensité ③

• One pair size 9 (5.5mm) needles OR SIZE TO OBTAIN GAUGE

• Cable needle (cn)

• Two size 8 (5mm) double-pointed needles (dpns) for I-cord ties

• Size I/9 (5.5mm) crochet hook

GAUGE
21 sts and 22 rows = 4"/10cm over cable rib pat using size 9 (5.5mm) needles. TAKE TIME TO CHECK GAUGE.

STITCH GLOSSARY
4-st RC Sl 2 sts to cn and hold to back, k2, k2 from cn.

CABLE RIB PATTERN

(over a multiple of 10 sts plus 4)

Row 1 (RS) K4, *p2, k2, p2, k4; rep from * to end.

Row 2 P4, *k2, p2, k2, p4; rep from * to end.

Row 3 Rep row 1.

Row 4 Rep row 2.

Row 5 4-st RC, *p2, k2, p2, 4-st RC;

rep from * to end.

Row 6 Rep row 2.

Row 7 Rep row 1.

Row 8 Rep row 2.

Rep rows 5–8 for cable rib pat.

HOOD

Cast on 104 sts. Work in cable rib pat until piece measures 9"/23cm from beg, end with a WS row. Bind off in rib.

FINISHING

Fold piece in half, RS tog. Sew cast-on edges tog for back seam. Bound-off edge is front edge of hood.

Picot edging and pompom ties

With hook, crochet a 3"/7.5cm chain for first pompom tie; with RS of bound-off edge facing, cont picot edging as foll: sc in first st of bound-off edge, *work [sc, ch 3, sc] in next st, skip next st, sc in next st; rep from * to last 3 sts, end work [sc, ch 3, sc] in next st, skip next st, sc in last st, crochet a 3"/7.5cm chain for 2nd pompom tie. Fasten off.

I-cord ties (make 2)

With dpn, cast on 4 sts, leaving a long tail for sewing. Work in I-cord as foll:

*Next row (RS) With 2nd dpn, k4, do not turn. Slide sts back to beg of needle to work next row from RS; rep from * for 14½"/37cm. Cut yarn, leaving a 6"/15cm tail, and thread through rem sts. Pull tog tightly, then secure end on inside. Tie this end in an overhand knot close to end. Sew opposite end of I-cord to first picot at bottom corner of hood. Sew 2nd tie to last picot at bottom corner of hood.

Pompoms

For crochet ties, make two 1½"/4cm pom poms. Sew pom poms to ends of ties. For top of hood, make a 2½"/6.5cm pom pom. Push top point of hood 2"/5cm to inside, then sew pom pom to center of crease to secure. ■

Diamond Cable Aviator Hat

Deborah Newton's high-crowned aviator hat is a little Amelia Earhart, a little Princess Anastasia. The diamond-cabled back flap covers the neck and ears; pompoms on the ties echo the one on the regally textured crown.

SIZE

Instructions are written for one size.

KNITTED MEASUREMENTS

Head circumference 21"/53.5cm
Length 13"/33cm

MATERIALS

• 3 3½oz/100g hanks (each approx 145yd/136m) Alpaca with a Twist *Highlander* (alpaca/wool/microfiber/viscose) in #0096 birch (4)

• One pair size 8 (5mm) needles OR SIZE TO OBTAIN GAUGE

• One size 8 (5mm) circular needle, 16"/40cm long

• One set (6) size 8 (5mm) double-pointed needles (dpns)

• Cable needle

• Stitch markers

GAUGE

18 sts and 28 rows = 4"/10cm over double moss st using size 8 (5mm) needles.
TAKE TIME TO CHECK GAUGE.

STITCH GLOSSARY

3-st RC Sl next st to cn and hold to *back*, k2, k1 from cn.

3-st LC Sl 2 sts to cn and hold to *front*, k1, k2 from cn.

4-st RC Sl 2 sts to cn and hold to *back*, k2, k2 from cn.

4-st LC Sl 2 sts to cn and hold to *front*, k2, k2 from cn.

DOUBLE MOSS STITCH (multiple of 4 sts)

Rnds 1 and 2 *K2, p2; rep from * around.
Rnds 3 and 4 *P2, k2; rep from * around.
Rep rnds 1–4 for double moss stitch.

HAT

Back flap

With size 8 (5mm) needle, cast on 50 sts. P 1 row.

Beg chart 1

Row 1 K1 to repeat line, work 12-st rep 3 times, work last 13 sts of chart. There will be 4 diamonds centered on flap. Work as established until row 10 has been completed.

Row 11 K3 to repeat line, work 12-st rep 3 times, work last 11 sts of chart. Work next row as established.

Row 13 K1 to repeat line, work 12-st rep 3 times, work last 13 sts of chart. Work as established until row 22 has been completed. Piece measures approx 3"/7.5cm. Bind off loosely.

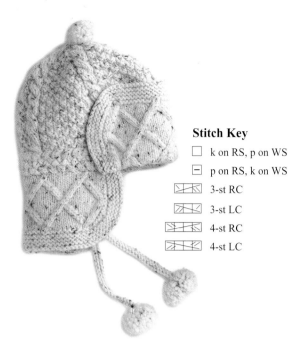

Stitch Key

☐ k on RS, p on WS

⊟ p on RS, k on WS

▱ 3-st RC

▱ 3-st LC

▱ 4-st RC

▱ 4-st LC

CHART 1

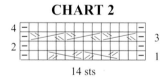

12-st rep

CHART 2

14 sts

CHART 3

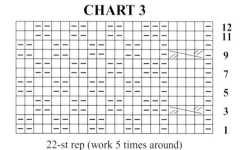

22-st rep (work 5 times around)

Back flap trim

Note Work into fabric by holding yarn on WS of work, and in same manner as picking up a st, insert point of knitting needle from RS through center of a st in knitted work, and pick up loop of yarn—1 st picked up.

With RS facing and circular needle, beg at bound-off edge and work along side edge, pick up and k 10 sts to center of widest part of full "diamond" (row 11 of the FIRST rep of the 22-row chart); work into the fabric, pick up and k 10 sts along the slanted side of the "diamond" to the first cross at the cast-on edge, so a triangle of St st folds back to the WS, pm; pick up and k 29 sts along cast-on edge to last cross, pm; work into the fabric as for other side, pick up and k 10 sts along the slanted side of the "diamond" to the side edge; pick up and k 10 sts along side edge to bound-off edge—69 sts. Do not join.

Next row (WS) Knit.

Next row (RS) K to marker, sl marker, M1, k to marker, M1, sl marker, k to end. Rep last 2 rows until there are 4 garter st ridges, end with a RS row. Bind off loosely knitwise.

Front flap

Work same as for back flap through chart row 22, then rep rows 3–12 once more. Bind off. Piece measures approx 5"/12.5cm.

Front flap trim

Place markers on each side at 1½"/4cm from bound-off edge. With RS facing and circular needle, beg at marker, work along side edge, pick up and k 14 sts to center of widest part of full "diamond"; pick up and k 10 sts along the slanted side of the "diamond" to the first cross at the cast-on edge, so a triangle of St st folds back to WS, pm; pick up and k 31 sts along cast-on edge to last cross, pm; work into the fabric as for other side, pick up and k 10 sts along the slanted side of the "diamond" to the side edge; pick up and k 14 sts along side edge to marker—79 sts. Do not join. Complete as for back flap trim.

Horizontal cable

With size 8 needles, cast on 14 sts.

Beg chart 2

Rep rows 1–4 of chart pat until cable measures 21"/53.5 from beg, slightly stretched. Bind off.

Crown

Place 4 markers along one edge of horizontal cable to divide it into 5 equal sections of approx 4¼"/10.5cm each. Join ends, sewing seam. With RS of cable facing and dpns, beg at seam, pick up and k 22 sts evenly in each section, using a separate dpn for each section—110 sts. Place marker and join, knitting with 6th dpn.

Beg chart 3

Rnd 1 Work 22 sts of chart 3 five times around. Cont to work chart in this manner through rnd 12. Rep rnds 1–12 until hat measures 5"/12.5cm from lower edge of horizontal cable.

Crown shaping

Next (dec) rnd [Work 5 sts of chart row, p2tog, cont in pat to end of dpn] 5 times—21 sts on each dpn, 105 sts in rnd. Work 1 rnd even. Rep last 2 rnds 12 times more—9 sts on each dpn, 45 sts in rnd.

Next (dec) rnd [K2tog, k1] 3 times on each dpn—6 sts on each dpn, 30 sts in rnd. Knit 1 rnd.
Next rnd [SK2P] twice on each needle—2 sts on each dpn, 10 sts in rnd.
Next rnd *K2tog; rep from * around. Cut yarn, leaving a long tail, thread tail through rem 5 sts with tapestry needle.

FINISHING

Mark seam of horizontal band as center front of hat. Place marker opposite for center back of hat. Place markers 6½"/16.5cm from each side of center back marker. Pin untrimmed, bound-off edge of back flap between these 2 markers with both RS facing, centering at back center marker. Sew flap to band. Turn hat inside out. Pin the WS of the untrimmed edge of front flap to the WS of horizontal cable along the upper ridge formed by the sts picked up for the front of hat. Sew pieces together along this ridge, allowing the trim at sides to extend over the back flap trim. Overlap the extensions of front flap trim over the back flap trim and sew in place. Fold front flap out over the RS of front of hat. Try on hat and pin upper flap to desired placement. Sew in place.

Ties (make 2)

With size 8 needle, cast on 26 sts. Purl 1 row, then bind off knitwise. Steam.

Pompoms

Make 3 pompoms and steam. Sew one pompom to top of hat. Sew one pompom to end of each tie, and sew other end of tie to each triangle tip underneath back flap trim. ■

Cabled Watch Cap

Hats off to Norah Gaughan for designing this fun traveling-cable cap. The cables advance with every twist, creating a swirl of texture around your head.

SIZE
Instructions are written for one size.

KNITTED MEASUREMENTS
Head circumference 18"/45.5cm

MATERIALS
• 1 3.5oz/100g hank (each approx 174yd/160m) of Berroco, Inc. *Peruvia* (wool) in #7110 naranja (orange) (4)

• Size 9 (5.5mm) circular needle, 16"/40.5cm long, OR SIZE TO OBTAIN GAUGE

• One set (4) size 9 (5.5mm) double-pointed needles (dpns)

• Cable needle (cn)

• Stitch marker

GAUGE
18 sts and 24 rnds to 4"/10cm over St st using size 9 (5.5mm) circular needle.
TAKE TIME TO CHECK GAUGE.

STITCH GLOSSARY
8-st RPC Sl next 5 sts to cn and hold to *back*, k3, (k3, p2) from cn.
6-st RC Sl next 3 sts to cn and hold to *back*, k3, k3 from cn.

CAP
With circular needle, cast on 96 sts. Join, taking care not to twist sts on needle. Place marker for end of rnd and sl marker every rnd.
Rnds 1–5 *P6, k6; rep from * around. **Rnd 6** *P4, 8-st RPC; rep from * around. **Rnds 7–15** *P4, k6, p2; rep from * around. **Rnd 16** *P2, 8-st RPC, p2; rep from * around. **Rnds 17–25** *P2, k6, p4; rep from * around. **Rnd 26** *8-st RPC, p4; rep from * around.

Crown shaping
Note Change to dpns (dividing sts evenly among three needles) when there are too few sts on circular needle.
Rnd 27 (dec) *K6, p2tog, p4; rep from * around—88 sts. **Rnds 28–33** *K6, p5; rep from * around. **Rnd 34 (dec)** *K6, p2tog, p3; rep from * around—80 sts. **Rnd 35** *K6, p4; rep from * around. **Rnd 36** *6-st RC, p4; rep from * around.
Rnd 37 (dec) *K6, p2tog, p2; rep from * around—72 sts. **Rnd 38 (dec)** *K5, ssk, p2—64 sts.
Rnd 39 (dec) *K5, ssk, p1—56 sts. **Rnd 40 (dec)** *K5, ssk—48 sts. **Rnd 41 (dec)** *K4, k2tog—40 sts.
Rnd 42 (dec) *K3, k2tog—32 sts. **Rnd 43 (dec)** *K2, k2tog—24 sts. **Rnd (dec) 44** *K1, k2tog—16 sts.
Rnd 45 (dec) [K2tog] 8 times—8 sts. Cut yarn, leaving an 8"/20.5cm tail, and thread through rem sts. Pull tog tightly and secure end. ■

Cabled Pillbox

Mari Tobita's smart topper is composed of a cabled panel knit sideways and trimmed with I-cord, then attached to a separately knit top. With six different criss-crossing patterns, it's a cable knitter's dream!

SIZES

Instructions are written for sizes Small/Medium (Large); shown in size Large.

KNITTED MEASUREMENTS

Top circumference approx 19 (21)"/48 (53)cm
Cabled panel length approx 20 (22)"/51 (56)cm
Cabled panel width 6¼"/10cm

MATERIALS

• 1 (1) 3½oz/100g hank (each approx 241yd/220m) of Fyberspates *Scrumptious DK/Worsted* (wool/silk) in #104 plum (4)

• One pair size 6 (4mm) needles
OR SIZE TO OBTAIN GAUGE

• One set (5) size 6 (4mm) double-pointed needles (dpns)

• Cable needle (cn)

• Tapestry needle

• 3 ¾"/2cm buttons

GAUGE

22½ sts and 32 rows = 4"/10cm over St st using size 6 needles.
37 sts and 34 rows = 4"/10cm over cable panel using size 6 needles.
TAKE TIME TO CHECK GAUGES.

ATTACHED I-CORD

With dpn, cast on 3 sts. With RS of hat facing, *pick up and k 1 edge st, slide sts to opposite end of needle and k2, ssk; rep from * to end.

STITCH GLOSSARY

kfb Knit into front and back of stitch.
4-st RPC Sl 1 st to cn and hold in *back*, k3, p1 from cn.
4-st LPC Sl 3 sts to cn and hold in *front*, p1, k3 from cn.
5-st RPC Sl 2 sts to cn and hold in *back*, k3, p2 from cn.
5-st LPC Sl 3 sts to cn and hold in *front*, p2, k3 from cn.
6-st RPC Sl 3 sts to cn and hold in *back*, k3, p3 from cn.
6-st LPC Sl 3 sts to cn and hold in *front*, p3, k3 from cn.
6-st RC Sl 3 sts to cn and hold in *back*, k3, k3 from cn.
6-st LC Sl 3 sts to cn and hold in *front*, k3, k3 from cn.

SHORT ROW WRAP & TURN (W&T)

[on RS row (on WS row)]
1) Wyib (wyif), sl next st purlwise.
2) Move yarn between the needles to the front (back).

3) Sl the same st back to LH needle. Turn work. One st is wrapped.

4) When working the wrapped st, insert RH needle under the wrap and work it tog with the corresponding st on needle.

HAT

Top

Cast 8 sts onto one dpn. Turn.

Next row (RS) Kfb in each st—16 sts.

Place 4 sts on each of 4 dpns, join and place marker (pm) for beg of rnd.

Next rnd [K2, pm, k2] over each dpn.

Next (inc) rnd [Kfb, k to marker, slip marker (sm), kfb, k to end] over each dpn—2 sts inc'd each dpn.

Next rnd Knit.

Rep last 2 rnds 10 (11) times more—26 (28) sts each dpn. Top measures approx 19 (21)"/ 48 (53)cm around. Bind off.

Cabled panel

With straight needles, cast on 47 sts.

Next row (WS) K1 (selvage st), k1, p3, k2, p3, k7, p6, k7, p3, k2, p3, k1, p1, k1, p5, k1 (selvage st).

Beg chart

Row 1 Work chart row 1—49 sts.

Work chart rows 2 and 3—51 sts.

Cont to follow chart until row 39 is complete.

Short rows 40 and 41 Work to end of short row, w&t, work to st 51.

Short rows 42 and 43 Work to end of short row, w&t, work to st 51.

Row 44 Work over all 51 sts, hiding wraps.

Cont to follow chart until row 48 is complete, rep rows 5—48 three times more, then work until shorter side edge (beg of RS rows) is 1"/2.5cm longer than circumference of crown top—approx 20 (22)"/51 (56)cm. Bind off.

FINISHING

Block pieces.

With dpns, beg at shorter side edge of bound-off row (beg of RS rows) and work attached I-cord all around cabled panel, except for bound-off edge. Beg with bound-off edge, pin cabled panel around edge of top, leaving 1"/2.5cm of cast-on edge free. Overlap cast-on edge on bound-off edge, pin in place. Sew pieces together, sew ends of cabled panel in place. Evenly space 3 buttons in a row at ½"/1cm in from cast-on edge and sew on through all layers. ■

48
short row 42
short row 40

47 sts, inc to 51 sts

short row 43
short row 41

47
45

rep rows 5–48

Stitch Key

- ☐ k on RS, p on WS
- ⊟ p on RS, k on WS
- Ⓜ make 1
- Ⓠ k1tbl
- ▨ no stitch
- 4-st RPC
- 4-st LPC
- 5-st RPC
- 5-st LPC
- 6-st RPC
- 6-st LPC
- 6-st RC
- 6-st LC

Rising Vines Beret

Anna Al's elegant slouchy beret features an intricate lacy vine motif, which emerges from an eyelet rib band. The amber-hued yarn gives off a rich glow.

SIZE
Instructions are written for one size.

KNITTED MEASUREMENTS
Brim circumference (stretched) approx 20"/51cm
Diameter 11½"/29cm

MATERIALS
• 1 3½oz/100g hank (each approx 450yd/411m) of Classic Elite *Alpaca Sox Kettle Dyes* (alpaca/merino wool/nylon) in #1830 bright amber ❶

• One size 3 (3.25mm) circular needle, 16"/40cm long, OR SIZE TO OBTAIN GAUGE

• One set (4) size 3 (3.25mm) double-pointed needles (dpns)

• Stitch marker

GAUGE
28 sts and 34 rnds = 4"/10cm over St st using size 3 (3.25mm) needle.
TAKE TIME TO CHECK GAUGE.

NOTE
To work in the rnd, always read chart from right to left.

STITCH GLOSSARY
inc 1 P1, k1 in same st.

BERET

Brim
With circular needle, cast on 112 sts. Join and pm, taking care not to twist sts on needle.
Rnd 1 *P1, k2tog, yo, p2, yo, ssk; rep from * around.
Rnd 2 K the knit sts and yo's, and p the purl sts.
Rnd 3 *P1, yo, ssk, p2, k2tog, yo; rep from * around.
Rnd 4 Rep rnd 2. Rep rnds 1–4 twice more.

Rise
Rnd 1 (inc) *P1, k2tog, yo, inc 1, k2tog, yo, k1, p1, k1, yo, ssk, inc 1, yo, ssk; rep from * around—128 sts.
Rnd 2 and all even rnds K the knit sts and yo's, and p the purl sts.
Rnd 3 (inc) *P1, yo, ssk, inc 1, k2tog, k2, yo, p1, yo, k2, ssk, inc 1, k2tog, yo; rep from * around—144 sts.
Rnd 5 (inc) *P1, k2tog, yo, inc 1, k2tog, k2, yo, k1, p1, k1, yo, k2, ssk, inc 1, yo, ssk; rep from * around—160 sts.
Rnd 7 (inc) *P1, yo, ssk, inc 1, k2tog, k2, yo, k2, p1, k2, yo, k2, ssk, inc 1, k2tog, yo, rep from * around—176 sts.
Rnd 9 (inc) *P1, k2tog, yo, inc 1, k2tog, k2, yo, k3, p1, k3, yo, k2, ssk, inc 1, yo, ssk, rep from * around—192 sts.

Beg chart pat

Rnd 1 Work 24-st rep 8 times. Cont to foll chart in this manner to rnd 32, then rep rnds 1–20 once more.

Crown shaping

Change to dpns (dividing sts evenly among 4 needles) when there are too few sts on circular needle.

Rnd 1 (dec) *P1, p2tog, yo, ssk, k1, k2tog, yo, p2, k2tog, yo, p1, yo, ssk, p2, yo, ssk, k1, k2tog, yo, p2tog; rep from * around—176 sts.

Rnd 2 *P3, k3, p3, k2, p1, k2, p3, k3, p2; rep from * around.

Rnd 3 (dec) *P3, k3tog, p2, k2tog, yo, k1, p1, k1, yo, ssk, p2, sssk, p2; rep from * around—144 sts.

Rnd 4 and all even rnds K the knit sts and yo's, and p the purl sts.

Rnd 5 (dec) *P2tog, p3, k2tog, k2, yo, p1, yo, k2, ssk, p4; rep from * around—136 sts.

Rnd 7 (dec) *P2, k2tog, k2, yo, k1, p1, k1, yo, k2, ssk, p2, p2tog; rep from * around—128 sts.

Rnd 9 *P1, k2tog, k2, yo, k2, p1, k2, yo, k2, ssk, p2; rep from * around.

Rnd 11 *K2tog, p2, yo, k3, p1, k3, yo, k2, ssk, p1; rep from * around.

Rnd 13 *K3, k2tog, k2, yo, p1, yo, k2, ssk, k3, p1; rep from * around.

Rnd 15 *K2, k2tog, k2, yo, k1, p1, k1, yo, k2, ssk, k2, p1; rep from * around.

Rnd 17 (dec) *Ssk, k1, k2tog, p5, ssk, k1, k2tog, p1; rep from * around—96 sts.

Rnd 19 (dec) *Sssk, p5, k3tog, p1; rep from * around—64 sts. Cut yarn, leaving a 10"/25.5cm tail, and thread through rem sts twice. Pull tog tightly and secure end. ∎

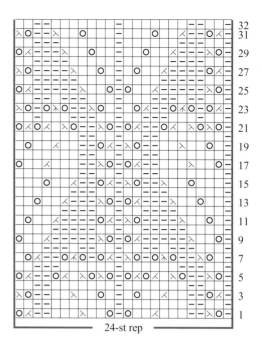

24-st rep

Stitch Key

☐ k
⊟ p
⊡ yo
⊠ k2tog
⊠ ssk
⊠ k3tog
⊠ sssk

Lace & Bobbles Beret

Jacqueline Jewett's romantic cap features lacy leaf motifs liberally sprinkled with bobbles on a reverse stockinette stitch background.

SIZE

Instructions are written for one size.

KNITTED MEASUREMENTS

Circumference approx 19"/48cm

Length approx 9"/23cm

MATERIALS

• 2 1¾oz/50g skeins (each approx 116yd/106m) of Debbie Bliss *Rialto DK* (merino) in #19 duck egg (3)

• One size 8 (5mm) circular needle, 32"/80cm long, OR SIZE TO OBTAIN GAUGE

• One size 6 (4mm) circular needle, 32"/80cm long

• Yarn needle

• Cable needle (cn)

GAUGE

20 sts and 26 rows = 4"/10cm over St st using larger needle. TAKE TIME TO CHECK GAUGE.

NOTE

Beret is worked back and forth in rows using circular needles.

STITCH GLOSSARY

Make bobble (MB) K1, p1, k1 into next stitch, turn, p3, turn, k3, turn, p3tog, turn, slip this st onto RH needle, pick up and k a stitch in the p3tog, and pass slipped st over picked-up st to anchor bobble.

RT K2tog, leaving sts on LH needle, then k the first st again, sl both sts off needle.

LT K the second st tbl, then k the first st and sl both sts off needle.

RPC Sl next st to cn and hold to *back,* k1, p1 from cn.

LPC Sl next st to cn and hold to *front,* p1, k1 from cn.

S2KP Sl 2 sts tog knitwise, k1, pass sl sts over k1.

BERET

With larger needles, cast on 7 sts for crown. Knit 2 rows.

Next (inc) row (RS) K1, [kfb] 5 times, k1—12 sts.

Next row Knit.

Next (inc) row K1, [kfb] 10 times, k1—22 sts.

Next row Knit.

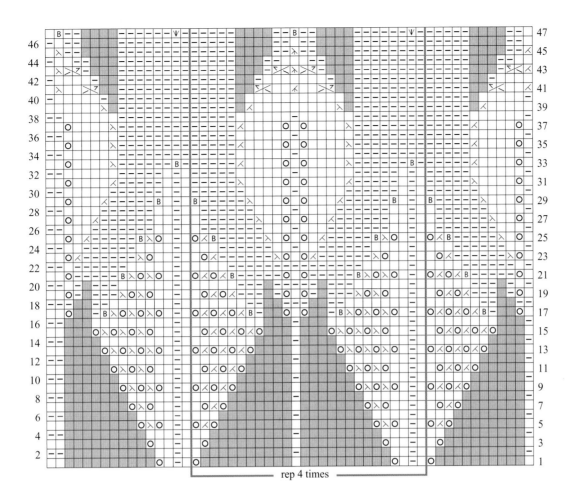

— rep 4 times —

Next row K1, [MB, k1] 10 times, k1.

Next row K1, p20, k1.

Beg chart

Row 1 (RS) Work to rep line, work rep 4 times, work to end of chart—32 sts.

Cont to work chart through row 47—102 sts.

Next row (WS) K10, p3, k1, [k16, p3, k1] 4 times, k8.

Next row K1, p7, [RT, k1, LT, p15] 4 times, RT, k1, LT, p8, k1.

Next row K9, p5, [k15, p5] 4 times, k8.

Next row K1, p7, [LPT, k1, RPT, p15] 4 times, LPT, k1, RPT, p8, k1.

Next row K10, p3, k1, [k16, p3, k1] 4 times, k8.

Next row K1, p7, [p1, SK2P, p16] 4 times, p1, SK2P, p9, k1—92 sts.

Stitch Key

☐ k on RS, p on WS		⤬ RPC
⊟ p on RS, k on WS		⤬ LPC
O yo		⤬ RT
⟋ k2tog		⤬ LT
⟍ ssk		⅄ SK2P
B make bobble		⟋ k3tog
Ⓥ k into front, back, and front of st		▦ no stitch

Next row (WS) Knit.

Next row Purl.

Next row Knit.

Change to smaller circular needle, knit 4 rows for garter st. Bind off loosely.

FINISHING

Sew back seam, matching lace motifs. ■

Star Flower Beanie

Lisa Craig's pretty topper is knit from the top down, beginning with a lacy six-petal flower motif, which forms the focus of the hat.

SIZES

Instructions are written for size X-Small/Small (Medium/Large); shown in size X-Small/Small.

KNITTED MEASUREMENTS

Circumference approx 19½ (21¾)"/49.5 (55)cm
Length approx 7 (8)"/18 (20.5)cm

MATERIALS

• 2 (2) 1¾oz/50g balls (each approx 110yd/100m) of Louisa Harding/KFI *Grace Hand-Dyed* (merino wool/silk) in #23 velvet (3)

• One each sizes 4 and 6 (3.5 and 4mm) circular needles, 16"/40cm long, OR SIZE TO OBTAIN GAUGE

• One set (5) size 6 (4mm) double-pointed needles (dpns)

• Stitch marker

GAUGE

22 sts and 34 rnds = 4"/10cm over St st using larger needle. TAKE TIME TO CHECK GAUGE.

NOTE Beanie is made from the top down.

STITCH GLOSSARY

inc 2 Work [k1, yo, k1] in same st.

BEANIE

Beg at center top, make a sl knot and place on dpn. With 2nd dpn, work [k1, p1] 6 times into sl knot—12 sts. Divide sts among 4 needles. Join, taking care not to twist sts on needles, pm for beg of rnds.

Crown shaping

Rnd 1 and all odd rnds Knit. **Rnd 2 (inc)** [Yo, k1] 12 times—24 sts. **Rnd 4 (inc)** [K2, inc 2, k1] 6 times—36 sts. **Rnd 6 (inc)** [K3, inc 2, k2] 6 times—48 sts. **Rnd 8 (inc)** [K4, inc 2, k3] 6 times—60 sts. **Rnd 10 (inc)** [K5, inc 2, k4] 6 times—72 sts. **Rnd 12 (inc)** [K6, inc 2, k5] 6 times—84 sts. Change to larger circular needle. **Rnd 14 (inc)** [K7, inc 2, k6] 6 times—96 sts. **Rnd 16 (inc)** [K8, inc 2, k7] 6 times—108 sts. **Rnd 17** Knit. For Medium/Large size only: **Rnd 18 (inc)** [K9, inc 2, k8] 6 times—120 sts. **Rnd 19** Knit.

Rise

Rnd 1 [K1, yo, ssk, k 13 (15), k2tog, yo] 6 times. **Rnd 2 and all even rnds** Knit. **Rnd 3** [K2, yo, ssk, k 11 (13), k2tog, yo, k1] 6 times. **Rnd 5** [K3, yo, ssk, k 9 (11), k2tog, yo, k2] 6 times. **Rnd 7** [K4, yo, ssk, k 7 (9), k2tog, yo, k3] 6 times. **Rnd 9** [K5, yo, ssk, k 5 (7), k2tog, yo, k4] 6 times. **Rnd 11** [K6, yo, ssk, k 3 (5), k2tog, yo, k5] 6 times. **Rnd 13** [K7, yo, ssk, k 1 (3), k2tog, yo, k6] 6 times. **Rnd 14** Knit.
For X-Small/Small size only: Rnd 15 [K8, yo, S2KP, yo, k7] 6 times. **For Medium/Large size only: Rnd 15** [K8, yo, ssk, k1, k2tog, yo, k7] 6 times. **Rnd 17** [K9, yo, S2KP, yo, k8] 6 times. **For all sizes** Cont in St st (knit every rnd) until piece measures 6 (7)"/15 (18)cm from beg. Change to smaller circular needle and cont in garter st (k 1 rnd, p 1 rnd) for 1"/2.5cm, end with a p rnd. Bind off loosely knitwise. ■

Wide-Brim Sun Hat

*Have your fun in the sun and keep your cool with this ice-blue sun hat
by Linda Medina. The eyelet pattern makes it light and airy.*

SIZE
Instructions are written for one size.

KNITTED MEASUREMENTS
Crown circumference approx 25"/63.5cm
Length approx 6¼"/16cm
Brim diameter 16"/40.5cm

MATERIALS
• 3 1¾oz/50g balls (each approx 137yd/125m) of Classic Elite *Soft Linen* (linen/wool/baby alpaca) in #2204 titan blue (3)

• One each sizes 5 and 8 (3.75 and 5mm) circular needles, 16"/40cm long, OR SIZE TO OBTAIN GAUGES

• One set (5) size 8 (5mm) double-pointed needles (dpns)

• Stitch marker

• Sewing needle and matching sewing thread

• 50"/127cm length of 19-gauge steel millinery wire covered with white rayon thread

• One plastic wire joiner

• Four ¾"/19mm bulldog clips

GAUGES
20 sts and 32 rnds = 4"/10cm over brim pat st using 1 strand of yarn and smaller needle.

16 sts and 24 rnds = 4"/10cm over crown pat st using 2 strands of yarn held tog and larger needle.
TAKE TIME TO CHECK GAUGES.

NOTES
1) Brim is worked using 1 strand of yarn.
2) Crown is worked using 2 strands of yarn held tog.

HAT
With smaller needle and 1 strand of yarn, cast on 240 sts. Join and pm, taking care not to twist sts on needle.

Hem
Rnds 1 and 2 Purl.
Rnd 3 Knit.

Brim
Rnd 1 *P3, yo, k3tog, yo; rep from * around.
Rnd 2 *K3, p3; rep from * around.
Rnd 3 *Yo, k3tog, yo, p3; rep from * around.
Rnd 4 *P3, k3; rep from * around.
Rnds 5-7 Rep rnds 1–3.
Rnd 8 (dec) *P3, k2tog, k1; rep from * around—200 sts.
Rnd 9 *P3, k2tog, yo; rep from * around.
Rnd 10 *K3, p2; rep from * around.
Rnd 11 *Yo, k3tog, yo, p2; rep from * around.
Rnd 12 *P3, k2; rep from * around.
Rnds 13-15 Rep rnds 9–11.
Rnd 16 (dec) *P3, SKP; rep from * around—160 sts.

Rnd 17 *P3, k1; rep from * around.

Rnd 18 *K3, p1; rep from * around.

Rnd 19 *Yo, k3tog, yo, p1; rep from * around.

Rnd 20 *P3, k1; rep from * around.

Rnds 21-23 Rep rnds 17–19.

Rnd 24 (dec) *P2, p2tog, k2, k2tog; rep from * around—120 sts.

Rnds 25-31 Rep rnds 1–7.

Rnd 32 (dec) *P3, k1, k2tog; rep from * around—100 sts. Change to larger needle and 2 strands of yarn held tog.

Crown

Rnd 1 *K3, yo (wrap yarn from back, over needle to front, then to back), k2tog; rep from * around.

Rnd 2 *K3, p1, k1; rep from * around.

Rnd 3 *K3, yo, k2tog; rep from * around.

Rnd 4 *K4, p1; rep from * around.

Rnds 5-16 Rep rnds 1–4 three times.

Crown shaping

Change to dpns (dividing sts evenly among 4 needles) when there are too few sts on circular needle.

Rnd 17 (dec) *K1, k2tog, yo, k2tog; rep from * around—80 sts.

Rnd 18 *K2, p1, k1; rep from * around.

Rnd 19 *K2, yo, k2tog; rep from * around.

Rnd 20 *K3, p1; rep from * around.

Rnd 21 Rep rnd 19.

Rnd 22 (dec) *K2tog, p1, k1; rep from * around—60 sts.

Rnd 23 *K1, yo, k2tog; rep from * around.

Rnd 24 *K2, p1; rep from * around.

Rnd 25 Rep rnd 23.

Rnd 26 Rep rnd 24.

Rnd 27 Rep rnd 23.

Rnd 28 (dec) *K2tog, p1; rep from * around—40 sts.

Rnd 29 *Yo, k2tog; rep from * around.

Rnd 30 *K1, p1; rep from * around.

Rnd 31 Rep rnd 29.

Rnd 32 Rep rnd 30.

Rnd 33 Rep rnd 29.

Rnd 34 (dec) *K2tog; rep from * around—20 sts.

Rnd 35 Rep rnd 29.

Rnd 36 Rep rnd 30.

Rnd 37 Rep rnd 29.

Rnd 38 Rep rnd 30.

Rnd 39 (dec) [K2tog] 10 times—10 sts. Cut yarns, leaving 8"/20.5cm tails, and thread through rem sts. Pull tog tightly and secure end.

FINISHING

To relax wire, run the wire back and forth around a round wooden chair or table leg a few times. Form wire into a 48"/122cm circumference circle, overlapping ends 2"/5cm and fastening them together using plastic joiner. Using tape measure and pencil, measure and mark wire every 12"/30.5cm. Fold hat brim in half, then yarn-mark each fold. Fold brim in half, matching yarn markers, then yarn-mark each fold. Place WS of brim on wire, matching yarn markers with pencil marks. Clip in place at each mark. With WS facing, use sewing needle and thread to secure wire to rnd 3 of hem with a few whipstitches. To secure wire to brim, work buttonhole stitches following rnd 3, spacing them stitches approx ½"/1.5cm apart. To cover wire, fold hem over to WS and sew in place. ■

Half Medallion Beret

Mari Tobita's luxurious beret is worked in three pieces: Two lace semicircles form the sides and are joined in the middle by a ribbed gusset. A ribbed band provides the finishing touch.

SIZES

Instructions are written for size Small/Medium (Large/X-Large); shown in size Small/Medium.

KNITTED MEASUREMENTS

Circumference approx 20 (21½)"/51 (54.5)cm
Length approx 8 (8½)"/20.5 (21.5)cm

MATERIALS

• 1 (1) 2oz/55g hank (each approx 200yd/183m) of Jade Sapphire *Mongolian Cashmere 4-Ply* (cashmere) in #089 sock eye ⟨3⟩

• One pair size 4 (3.5mm) needles
OR SIZE TO OBTAIN GAUGE

• One size 3 (3.25mm) circular needle, 16"/40cm long

• Stitch marker

GAUGE

27 sts and 37 rows = 4"/10cm over St st using size 4 (3.5mm) needles.
Half medallion = 8"/20.5cm wide x 4½"/11.5cm high, using size 4 (3.5mm) needles.
TAKE TIME TO CHECK GAUGE.

NOTES

1) Beret is made in 3 pieces (2 half medallions and one gusset), then sewn tog.
2) Ribbed band is added after beret is assembled.

STITCH GLOSSARY

pfb Inc 1 by purling into the front and back of the next st.

kfb Inc 1 by knitting into the front and back of the next st.

MB (make bobble) Work as foll:
Row 1 (WS) Work [yo, p1] 3 times in same st, making 6 sts from one. Turn.
Rows 2 and 4 Sl 1, k5. Turn.
Rows 3 and 5 Sl 1, p5. Turn.
Row 6 [K2tog] 3 times—3 sts. Turn.
Row 7 P3tog—1 st. Do not turn.

HALF MEDALLIONS (MAKE 2)

With straight needles, cast on 5 sts.

Row 1 (RS) K5.

Row 2 P4, pfb, pick up and purl 1 st in side edge—7 sts.

Row 3 K6, kfb, pick up and knit 1 st in side edge—9 sts.

Row 4 K1 (selvage st), p7, k1 (selvage st).

Row 5 K3, [yo, k1] 4 times, k2—13 sts.

Row 6 K1, p to last st, k1.

Row 7 K2, k1tbl, [yo, k3, yo, k1tbl] twice, k2—17 sts.

Row 8 Rep row 6.

Row 9 K2, k1tbl, [yo, k5, yo, k1tbl] twice, k2—21 sts.

Row 10 K1, p1, [MB, p3] 4 times, MB, p1, k1.

Row 11 K3, [yo, k7, yo, k1] twice, k2—25 sts.

Row 12 and all foll WS rows K1, p to last st, k1.

Row 13 K3, [yo, ssk, k2tog, yo, k1] 4 times, k2.

Row 15 K3, [k1, yo, k2tog, yo, k2] 4 times, k2—29 sts.

Row 17 K3, [k2, yo, k1tbl, yo, k3] 4 times, k2—37 sts.

Row 19 K3, [k3, yo, k1tbl, yo, k4] 4 times, k2—45 sts.

Row 21 K3, [k4, yo, k1tbl, yo, k5] 4 times, k2—53 sts.

Row 23 K3, [k5, yo, k1tbl, yo, k6] 4 times, k2—61 sts.

Row 25 K3, [k6, yo, k1tbl, yo, k7] 4 times, k2—69 sts.

Row 27 K3, [k7, yo, k1tbl, yo, k8] 4 times, k2—77 sts.

Row 29 K2, p1, [ssk, k5, yo, k3, yo, k5, k2tog, p1] 4 times, k2.

Row 31 K2, p1, [ssk, k4, yo, k5, yo, k4, k2tog, p1] 4 times, k2.

Row 33 K2, p1, [ssk, k3, yo, k1, yo, ssk, k1, k2tog, yo, k1, yo, k3, k2tog, p1] 4 times, k2.

Row 35 K2, p1, [ssk, k2, yo, k3, yo, SK2P, yo, k3, yo, k2, k2tog, p1] 4 times, k2.

Row 37 K2, p1, [ssk, k1, yo, k11, yo, k1, k2tog, p1] 4 times, k2.

Row 39 K2, p1, [ssk, yo, (k1, yo, ssk, k1, k2tog, yo) twice, k1, yo, k2tog, p1] 4 times, k2.

Row 41 K2, ssk, yo, [k3, yo, SK2P, yo] 11 times, k3, yo, ssk, k2. Bind off purlwise on WS row.

GUSSET

With straight needles, cast on 35 (41) sts.

Row 1 (RS) K1 (selvage st), [k3, p3] 5 (6) times, k3, k1 (selvage st).

Row 2 K1, [p3, k3] 5 (6) times, p3, k1. Rep rows 1 and 2 until piece measures 14"/35.5cm, end with a RS row. Bind off in rib pat.

FINISHING

Block half medallions to measurements. Sew side edges of gusset to curved edges of half medallions.

Ribbed band

With RS facing and circular needle, pick up and knit 50 sts along bottom edge of first half medallion, 17 (23) sts along first gusset edge, 50 sts along bottom edge of 2nd half medallion, then 17 (23) sts along 2nd gusset edge—134 (146) sts. Join and pm for beg of rnds. Work around in k1, p1 rib for 1 (1½)"/2.5 (4)cm. Bind off loosely in rib. ■

Leaf Lace Beret

You don't have to be a detective to figure out that there's nothing more fetching than a beret. Kate Gagnon Osborn is on the case with this lacy version.

SIZE

Instructions are written for one size.

KNITTED MEASUREMENTS

Brim circumference (unstretched) approx 17"/43cm
Diameter 10"/25.5cm

MATERIALS

• 1 3½oz/100g hank (each approx 440yd/402m) of Tilli Tomas *Artisan Sock* (superwash merino/nylon) in norse #84 ①

Note Yarn used in original pattern is no longer available. Original yarn is listed on page 175.

• One size 2 (2.75mm) circular needle, 20"/50cm long, OR SIZE TO OBTAIN GAUGE

• One set (5) size 2 (2.75mm) double-pointed needles (dpns)

• Size 0 (2mm) circular needle, 16"/40cm long

• Stitch marker

GAUGES

28 sts and 35 rnds = 4"/10cm over St st using larger needles, after blocking.
30 sts and 38 rnds = 4"/10cm over chart pat using larger needles, after blocking.
TAKE TIME TO CHECK GAUGES.

BERET

With smaller needle, cast on 140 sts, pm and join, being careful not to twist.

Next rnd *[K1, p1] twice, k1, p2; rep from * around.
Rep last rnd until piece measures 1"/2.5cm.

Next (inc) rnd *[K1, yo, p1, yo] twice, k1, p2; rep from * around—220 sts.

Next rnd *[K1, k1 tbl, p1, p1 tbl] twice, k1, p2; rep from * around.

Beg chart

Change to larger needles. Work 11-st rep of chart 20 times around. Work chart through rnd 60, changing to dpns when sts no longer fit comfortably on circular needle. When chart is complete there will be 40 sts on needles.

Next (dec) rnd *SKP; rep from * to end—20 sts. Rep last rnd once more—10 sts. Cut yarn, leaving 8"/20.5cm tail. Thread tail through rem sts.

FINISHING

To block, soak beret in warm water and wool wash. Stretch over a 10"/25.5cm plate to dry. ∎

Stitch Key

☐	k
⊟	p
⊙	yo
⊠	k2tog
⊠	skp
⊠	p2tog

Chart rows numbered: 1, 3, 5, 7, 9, 11, 13, 15, 17, 19, 21, 23, 25, 27, 29, 31, 33, 35, 37, 39, 41, 43, 45, 47, 49, 51, 53, 55, 57, 59, 60

← 11-st rep →
(work 20 times around)

Lace Toque

Reminiscent of a classic chef's hat, Lisa Daehlin's spunky topper features a deep ribbed band that folds back into a cuff and a lace crown that forms a square shape. It's a recipe for fun!

SIZE

Instructions are written for one size.

KNITTED MEASUREMENTS

Brim circumference 22"/56cm
Length 10"/25.5cm

MATERIALS

• 2 3½oz/100g balls (each approx 186yd/170m) of Rowan/Westminster Fibers, Inc., *Pure Wool Aran* (superwash wool) in #686 vert (4)

• One set (5) each size 6 (4mm) double-pointed needles (dpns) OR SIZE TO OBTAIN GAUGE

• One set (5) size 8 (5mm) dpns

• Size 8 (5mm) circular needle, 24"/60cm long

• Stitch markers

GAUGE

22 sts and 28 rnds to 4"/10cm over k2, p2 rib slightly stretched, using smaller needles.
TAKE TIME TO CHECK YOUR GAUGE.

NOTES

1) Pattern st is worked a total of 30 times around.
2) Beg of rnd is moved in rnds 18 and 20.

K2, P2 RIB

(multiple of 4 sts)
Rnd 1 *K2, p2; rep from * around.
Rnd 2 K the knit sts and p the purl sts.
Rep rnd 2 for k2, p2 rib.

TOQUE

With smaller needles, cast on 120 sts. Place marker (pm) for beg of rnd and join, being careful not to twist sts. Work in k2, p2 rib until piece measures 5"/12.5cm.
Next (inc) rnd K1, *yo, k4; rep from * around, end yo, k3—150 sts.
Change to larger needles.
Next rnd Knit.

Beg pat st

Rnd 1 K1, *yo, k1, yo, k4; rep from * around, end last rep k3 (instead of k4)—210 sts.
Rnd 2 and all even rnds through rnd 16 Knit.
Rnd 3 K1, *yo, k3, yo, k4; rep from * around, end last rep k3—270 sts.
Rnd 5 K1, *yo, k5, yo, k4; rep from * around end last rep k3—330 sts.
Rnd 7 K1, *[yo, k1] twice, S2KP, [k1, yo] twice, k4;

rep from * around, end last rep k3—390 sts.

Rnd 9 K1, *yo, k3, yo, S2KP, yo, k3, yo, k4; rep from * around, end last rep k3—450 sts.

Rnd 11 K1, *yo, k1, [S2KP, yo] twice, S2KP, k1, yo, k4; rep from * around, end last rep k3—390 sts.

Rnd 13 K1, *yo, k3tog, [yo, S2KP] twice, yo, k4; rep from * around, end last rep k3—330 sts.

Rnd 15 k1, *yo, k2tog, S2KP, SKP, yo, k4; rep from * around, end last rep k3—270 sts.

Rnd 17 K1, *yo, k1, S2KP, k1, yo, k4; rep from * around, end last rep, k3—270 sts.

Rnd 18 Knit to last st, pm for new beg of rnd, remove old marker.

Rnd 19 *SKP, yo, S2KP, yo, k2tog, k2; rep from * around—210 sts.

Rnd 20 Rep rnd 18.

Rnd 21 *SKP, yo, SK2P, yo, k2tog; rep from * around—150 sts.

Rnd 22 Knit.

Rnd 23 *SKP, k1, k2tog; rep from * around—90 sts.

Shape top

Set-up rnd K11, pm in last st, k23, pm in last st, k21, pm in last st, k24, pm in last st, k to end.

Next (dec) rnd [K to 1 st before marked st, remove marker, S2KP, pm in this st] 4 times—8 sts dec'd.

Rep last rnd 8 times more—18 sts.

Change to smaller needles.

Rep dec rnd once more—10 sts.

Cut yarn leaving long tail. Thread tail through open sts twice. ∎

Sunflower Medallion Beret

Anna Al's beret-with-a-twist starts in the round from the sunflower medallion crown, progresses through the beautifully textured lacy rise, and finishes with a garter-stitch tied band, worked back and forth.

SIZE

Instructions are written for one size.

KNITTED MEASUREMENTS

Brim circumference approx 19"/48cm

Diameter 11"/28cm

MATERIALS

• 2 1¾oz/50g hanks (each approx 170yd/155m) of Koigu Wool Designs *KPPPM* (merino wool) in #P319X blues and purples (**1**)

• Size 3 (3.25mm) circular needle, 16"/40cm long, OR SIZE TO OBTAIN GAUGE

• One set (4) size 3 (3.25mm) double-pointed needles (dpns)

• Stitch marker

GAUGE

28 sts and 34 rnds = 4"/10cm over St st using size 3 (3.25mm) needle.
TAKE TIME TO CHECK GAUGE.

NOTE

Beret is made from the top down.

BERET

Crown shaping

Beg at center top, with dpns, cast on 8 sts.
Divide sts over 4 needles. Join, taking care not to twist sts on needles; pm for beg of rnds.
Rnd 1 (inc) *Yo, k1; rep from * around—16 sts.
Rnd 2 and all even rnds Knit.
Rnd 3 (inc) *Yo, k3, yo, k1; rep from * around—24 sts.
Rnd 5 (inc) *Yo, k5, yo, k1; rep from * around—32 sts.
Rnd 7 (inc) *Yo, k7, yo, k1; rep from * around—40 sts.
Rnd 9 *Yo, ssk, k2tog, yo, k1; rep from * around.
Rnd 11 (inc) *K1, yo, k2tog, yo, k2; rep from * around—48 sts.
Rnd 13 (inc) *K2, yo, k1, yo, k3; rep from * around—64 sts.
Rnd 15 (inc) *K3, yo, k1, yo, k4; rep from * around—80 sts.

Rnd 17 (inc) *K4, yo, k1, yo, k5; rep from * around—96 sts.

Rnd 19 (inc) *K5, yo, k1, yo, k6; rep from * around—112 sts. Change to circular needle.

Rnd 21 (inc) *K6, yo, k1, yo, k7, rep from * around—128 sts.

Rnd 23 (inc) *K7, yo, k1, yo, k8; rep from * around—144 sts.

Rnd 24 Knit.

Rise

Rnd 1 *K5, k2tog, yo, k3, yo, ssk, k6, rep from * around.

Rnd 2 and all even rnds Knit.

Rnd 3 *K4, k2tog, yo, k5, yo, ssk, k5; rep from * around.

Rnd 5 *K3, k2tog, yo, k1, yo, ssk, k1, k2tog, yo, k1, yo, ssk, k4; rep from * around.

Rnd 7 *K2, k2tog, yo, k3, yo, SK2P, yo, k3, yo, ssk, k3; rep from * around.

Rnd 9 *K1, k2tog, yo, k11, yo, ssk, k2; rep from * around.

Rnd 11 *K2tog, yo, k1, yo, [ssk, k1, k2tog, yo, k1, yo] twice, ssk, k1; rep from * around.

Rnd 13 K1, pm for new beg of rnd, *yo, k3, yo, SK2P; rep from * around.

Rnd 15 (inc) *Yo, k17, yo, k1; rep from * around—160 sts.

Rnd 17 (inc) *[Yo, k1, yo, ssk, k1, k2tog] 3 times, [yo, k1] twice; rep from * around—176 sts.

Rnd 19 (inc) *[Yo, k3, yo, SK2P] 3 times, yo, k3, yo, k1; rep from * around—192 sts.

Beg chart

Work 6-st rep of chart 32 times around until rnd 12 is complete, then work rnds 1–12 once more.

Stitch Key

□	knit
⟋	k2tog
⟍	ssk
O	yo
⋏	SK2P

*Rnd 11 K to end of rnd, remove marker, k1, pm for new beg of rnd.

Next rnd (dec) *K10, k2tog; rep from * around—176 sts.

Next rnd Knit.

Next rnd (dec) *K9, k2tog; rep from * around—160 sts.

Brim and ties

Working back and forth, work in garter st (k every row) as foll:

Next row Cast on 30 sts, k30, *k8, k2tog; rep from * to end—174 sts.

Next row Cast on 30 sts, k to end—204 sts.

Next row K30, [k7, k2tog] 16 times, k30—188 sts. Work even until garter brim measures 1¼"/3cm. Bind off knitwise ∎.

Plaid Tam

Take a virtual trip to bonny Scotland when you knit this charming tam complete with a perky pompom. Theresa Schabes's plaid pattern is not traditional, but captures the spirit of classic tartans.

SIZE

Instructions are written for one size.

KNITTED MEASUREMENTS

Brim circumference approx 19"/48cm
Diameter 11"/28cm

MATERIALS

• 1 1¾oz/50g ball (each approx 175yd/160m) of Rowan/Westminster Fibers *Cashsoft 4-Ply* (extrafine merino wool/acrylic microfiber/cashmere) each in #449 bottleblue (A), #460 pretty (B), #446 quartz (C), and #431 deep (D) **❶**

• One each sizes 3 and 4 (3.25 and 3.5mm) circular needles, 16"/40cm long, OR SIZE TO OBTAIN GAUGE

• One set (5) size 4 (3.5mm) double-pointed needles (dpns)

• Size G/6 (4mm) crochet hook

• Stitch markers

GAUGE

24 sts and 32 rnds = 4"/10cm over St st using larger needle. TAKE TIME TO CHECK GAUGE.

NOTES

1) Horizontal stripes are knitted in.
2) Vertical stripes are worked in slip stitch crochet after tam is completed.

STITCH GLOSSARY

sl st crochet (slip stitch crochet) Slip stitch crochet is worked over the vertical column of ladders that connect two stitches. To beg, insert crochet hook from RS to WS under ladder indicated in instructions. Using color stated, make a slip knot and place on hook, then use hook to draw slip knot to RS. Taking care to maintain row gauge, cont as foll: *insert hook under next ladder. Yo and draw loop to RS, then through loop on hook; rep from * to garter ridge of brim.

CORRUGATED RIB

(over a multiple of 4 sts)
Rnd 1 (RS) *K2 with B, k2 with C; rep from * around.
Rnds 2-4 *K2 with B, p2 with C; rep from * around.
Rnd 5 *K2 with C, k2 with D; rep from * around.
Rnd 6 *K2 with C, p2 with D; rep from * around.
Rnd 7 *K2 with B, k2 with C; rep from * around.
Rnds 8-10 *K2 with B, p2 with C; rep from * around.
Work rnds 1–10 for corrugated rib.

STRIPE PATTERN

Working in St st, *work 3 rnds B, 1 rnd D, 2 rnds B, 1 rnd A, 2 rnds B, 1 rnd D, 2 rnds B, 1 rnd C; rep from * (13 rnds) for stripe pat.

TAM

Brim

With smaller needle and A, cast on 120 sts. Join and pm, taking care not to twist sts on needle. Cut A. Work rnds 1–10 of corrugated rib.

Next (inc) rnd With C, *[k3, M1] twice, k4, M1; rep from * around—156 sts.

Next (garter ridge) rnd With C, purl. Change to larger needle.

Rise

Working in St st (knit every rnd) and stripe pat, work even until piece measures 5"/12.5cm from beg. Cont in stripe pat as established, work as foll:

Next rnd *K26, pm; rep from * around 5 times, end k26—6 st markers (including beg of rnd marker).

Crown shaping

Change to dpns (dividing sts evenly among 4 needles) when there are too few sts on circular needle.

Next (dec) rnd *Work to 3 sts before marker, k3tog; rep from * around—138 sts.

Next rnd Knit.

Next (dec) rnd *Work to 3 sts before marker, k3tog; rep from * around—120 sts.

Next rnd Knit. Cont to rep last 2 rnds 6 times more—12 sts.

Next (dec) rnd [K2tog] 6 times—6 sts. Cut yarn, leaving an 8"/20.5cm tail, and thread through rem sts twice. Pull tog tightly and secure end.

Cut rem colors and weave in on WS.

FINISHING

Vertical stripes

**With RS facing, and starting at center top of hat, insert crochet hook through top ladder to the right of a line of dec's. With C, make a slip knot and place on hook. Cont to work sl st crochet following line of dec's, then cont straight (when dec's end) to garter st ridge. For all stripes, cut yarn and draw through rem loop on hook, then weave in ends.

For 2nd vertical stripe, count 4 sts to the right of first vertical stripe. Here you will be working to the left of next line of dec's. Locate top ladder that's 4 sts from first vertical stripe. With RS facing, insert crochet hook through top ladder to the left of next line of dec's. With D, make a slip knot and place on hook. Cont to work sl st crochet straight to garter st ridge.

For 3rd vertical stripe, count 3 sts to the right of 2nd vertical stripe. Locate top ladder that's 3 sts from 2nd vertical stripe. Using A, cont to work as for 2nd stripe.

For 4th vertical stripe, count 3 sts to the right of 3rd vertical stripe. Locate top ladder that's 3 sts from 3rd vertical stripe. Using D, cont to work as for 2nd stripe.

For 5th vertical stripe, count 3 sts to the right of 4th vertical stripe. Locate top ladder that's 3 sts from 4th vertical stripe. Using C, cont to work as for 2nd stripe.

For 6th vertical stripe, count 3 sts to the right of 5th vertical stripe. Locate top ladder that's 3 sts from 4th vertical stripe. Using D, cont to work as for 2nd stripe.

For 7th vertical stripe, count 3 sts to the right of 6th vertical stripe. Locate top ladder that's 3 sts from fourth vertical stripe. Using A, cont to work as for 2nd stripe.

For 8th vertical stripe, count 3 sts to the right of 7th vertical stripe. Locate top ladder that's 3 sts from 7th vertical stripe. Using D, cont to work as for 2nd stripe**. Rep from ** to ** 5 times more.

To block, wet tam, then gently squeeze out water without wringing. Roll tam in a terry towel to absorb excess moisture. Insert an 11"/28cm dinner plate inside tam. Arrange tam evenly over plate. Invert a wide-bottomed glass on work surface, then place plate on top. Let dry.

Pompom

Make a 1¾"/4.5cm pompom using B and sew to top of tam. ■

Nordic Snowflake Tuque

A traditional stranded Norwegian design gets a modern update in Cheryl Murray's slouchy hat. A corrugated rib band leads to oversized snowflake motifs and a striped crown.

SIZE

Instructions are written for one size.

KNITTED MEASUREMENTS

Circumference approx 20"/51cm
Length 11"/28cm

MATERIALS

• 2 1¾oz/50g balls (each approx 114yd/105m) of Bergère de France *Origin Merinos* (merino wool) in #242.87 brasier (A) 🔢

• 1 ball each in #242.96 ardeur (B) and #242.74 cocon (C)

• One size 7 (4.5mm) circular needle, 16"/40cm long, OR SIZE TO OBTAIN GAUGE

• One set (5) size 7 (4.5mm) double-pointed needles (dpns)

• Stitch marker

GAUGE

24 sts and 26 rnds = 4"/10cm over chart pat using size 7 (4.5mm) needle.
TAKE TIME TO CHECK GAUGE.

NOTE

To work in the rnd, always read chart from right to left.

CORRUGATED RIB

(over a multiple of 4 sts)
Rnd 1 (RS) *K2 with B, p2 with A;
rep from * around.
Rep this rnd for corrugated rib.

STRIPE PATTERN

Working in St st, *work 2 rnds B, 2 rnds A;
rep from * (4 rnds) for stripe pat.

TUQUE

Brim

With circular needle and A, cast on 120 sts. Join and pm, taking care not to twist sts on needle. Work in corrugated rib for 2"/5cm. Cont in St st (knit every rnd) as foll:

Beg chart pat

Rnd 1 (RS) Work 40-st rep 3 times. Cont to foll chart in this way through rnd 47. Change to stripe pat and work even until 4 stripes (8 rnds) have been completed; piece should measure approx 9½"/24cm from beg.

Crown shaping

Change to dpns (dividing sts evenly among 4 needles) when there are too few sts on circular needle. Cont in stripe pat as established and work as foll:

Color Key
- ■ Brasier (A)
- ■ Ardeur (B)
- □ Cocon (C)

40-st rep

Rnd 1 (dec) *K10, k2tog; rep from * around—110 sts.

Rnds 2-4 Knit.

Rnd 5 (dec) *K9, k2tog; rep from * to end—100 sts.

Rnd 6 Knit.

Rnd 7 (dec) *K8, k2tog, rep from * to end—90 sts.

Rnd 8 Knit.

Rnd 9 (dec) *K7, k2tog, rep from * to end—80 sts.

Rnd 10 Knit.

Rnd 11 (dec) *K6, k2tog, rep from * to end—70 sts.

Rnd 12 (dec) *K5, k2tog, rep from * to end—60 sts.

Rnd 13 (dec) *K4, k2tog, rep from * to end—50 sts.

Rnd 14 Knit. Cut B, leaving a 10"/25.5cm tail, and thread through rem sts twice. Pull tog tightly and secure end. Cut A and weave in end on WS. ■

Striped Hood

Brenda Castiel's shaped, two-tone knit is a sleek take on the basic hood. Worked from the top to the shoulders, it features a subtle two-colored twisted-stitch pattern, framed in garter stitch.

SIZES
Instructions are written for sizes X-Small/Small (Medium/Large); shown in size X-Small/Small.

KNITTED MEASUREMENTS
Length approx 15"/38cm
Hood width at ear level approx
14 (15½)"/ 35.5 (40)cm

MATERIALS
- 2 (3) 1¾ oz/50g skeins (each approx 114yd/105m) of Bergère de France *Origin Merinos* (wool) in #243.00 veloute (purple) (MC) 4

- 1 (2) skeins in #242.98 entreinte (navy) (CC)

- Size 8 (5mm) circular needle, 24"/61cm long, OR SIZE TO OBTAIN GAUGE

- Size 7 (4.5mm) circular needle, 24"/61cm long

- Stitch markers

- 2 ¾"/2cm buttons

GAUGE
24 sts and 24 rows = 4"/10 cm over 2-color pattern using larger needles.
TAKE TIME TO CHECK GAUGE.

STITCH GLOSSARY

kfb Knit into front and back of st—1 st inc'd.

2-st RT K2tog without removing the stitches from LH needle, knit the first st again, then slip from needle.

2-COLOR PATTERN

(multiple of 4 sts plus 2)

Row 1 (RS) *K2CC, k2MC; rep from *, end k2CC.

Rows 2 and 4 *K2CC, p2MC; rep from *, end k2CC.

Row 3 *K2CC, 2-st RT with MC; rep from *, end k2CC.

Rep rows 1–4 for 2-color pattern.

HOOD

Top

With MC and larger needle, cast on 24 sts.

Beg 2-color pattern

Row 1 (RS) K1CC, work in pat to last 1 st, k1CC.

Row 2 K1CC, work in pat to last st, k1CC.

Keeping first and last CC sts of every row in garter st (knit every row), work even in pat until piece measures 5 (7)"/12.5 (18)cm from beg, end with a WS row.

Note Work decreases in pattern.

Next (dec) row (RS) Work 1 st, ssk, work in pat to last 3 sts, k2tog, k1—22 sts.

Next (dec) row (WS) Work 1 st, ssk, work in pat to last 3 sts, k2tog, k1—20 sts.

Next row Work even.

Next (dec) row (WS) Work 1 st, ssk, work in pat to last 3 sts, k2tog, k1—18 sts.

Next (dec) row (RS) Work 1 st, ssk, work in pat to last 3 sts, k2tog, k1—16 sts.

Next row Work even. Place sts on holder, cut yarn.

Sides

With CC and larger needle, cast on 1 st, then, with RS facing, beg at cast-on edge, pick up and knit 26 (30) sts along right side edge, k16 sts from holder, pick up and knit 26 (30) sts along left side edge, cast on 1 st—70 (78) sts.

Beg 2-color pattern

Next row (WS) Work row 2 of pat.

Work even until piece measures 7"/18cm from pickup row, end with a RS row.

Neck shaping

Next row (WS) Work 20 (24) sts, place marker (pm), work 30 sts, pm, work 20 (24) sts. Slip markers every row.

Next row (RS) Work to marker; [with CC, k2tog, with MC, work 2 sts in pat] 7 times, with CC, k2tog; work to end—62 (70) sts.

Next row (WS) Work to marker; [k1CC, with MC, work 2 sts] 7 times, k1CC; work to end. Work 2 rows even.

Next row (RS) Work to marker; [k1CC, with MC, k2tog] 7 times, k1CC; work to end—55 (63) sts.

Next row (WS) Work to marker, slip marker; [k1CC, p1MC] 7 times, k1CC; work to end.

Front shaping

Note Work increased sts into 2-color pattern.

Row 1 (RS) Kfb, work to last st, kfb—2 sts inc'd.

Row 2 Work even.

Row 3 Kfb, work to last st, kfb—2 sts inc'd.

Row 4 Work even.

Row 5 Kfb, work to last st, kfb—2 sts inc'd.

Row 6 (WS) Kfb, work to last st, kfb—63 (71) sts.

Repeat last 6 rows once more—71 (79) sts.

Repeat rows 1–4 once more—75 (83) sts.

Shoulders

Next row (RS) Work to marker, slip marker, [k1CC, with MC, kfb] 7 times, k1CC, work to end—82 (90) sts.

Work 3 rows even.

Next row (RS) Work to marker, slip marker, [with CC, kfb, with MC, work 2 sts] 7 times, with CC kfb, work to end—90 (98) sts. Remove markers.

Next row (WS) Work 14 (16) sts, pm, work 18 (20) sts, pm, work 26 sts, pm, work 18 (20) sts, pm, work 14 (16) sts.

Beg shoulder shaping

Note Work increased sts into 2-color pattern.

Next (inc) ro (RS) [Work to 1 st before marker, kfb, slip marker, kfb] 4 times, work to end— 98 (106) sts.

Next row Work even.

Rep last 2 rows 4 times more—130 (138) sts.

Hem

Next row (RS) With MC, knit.

Next row (WS) P1, *k to 1 st before marker, kfb, slip marker, kfb; rep from *, k to last st, p1—138 (146) sts.

Rep last 2 rows once more—146 (154) sts.

Next row (RS) Knit.

Next row (WS) P1, k to last st, p1.

Bind off loosely purlwise.

FINISHING

Edging

With RS facing, MC, and smaller needle, beg at bound-off end of right front, pick up and knit 30 (32) sts along angled edge, 36 sts along right side of hood, 24 sts along cast-on edge of top, 36 sts along left side of hood, 30 (32) sts along angled edge—156 (160) sts.

Next (buttonhole) row (WS) Sl 1 purlwise, k to last 14 sts, [bind off 3 sts, k4] twice.

Next row (RS) Sl 1 purlwise, k to end, casting on 3 sts over buttonholes.

Next row Sl 1 purlwise, k to end.

Next row Sl 1 purlwise, k21 (23) [k2tog, k9] 10 times, k2tog, k22 (24)—145 (149) sts.

Next row Sl 1 purlwise, k to end.

Bind off loosely purlwise.

Sew on buttons opposite buttonholes. ∎

Double-Knit Hat

Whether you're feeling blue or your mood is more mellow yellow, Elli Stubenrauch's playful "bird on a wire" design will double your fun. The charted portion is double-knit, while each layer of the crown is stitched separately.

SIZE
Instructions are written for one size.

KNITTED MEASUREMENTS
Circumference 21"/53.5cm
Length 8"/20.5cm

MATERIALS
• One 1¾oz/50g skein (each approx 185yd/169m) of Louet North America *Gems Fingering* (superwash wool) each in #56 navy (MC) and #65 goldenrod (CC) **1**

• One size 1 (2.25mm) circular needle, 20"/50cm long, OR SIZE TO OBTAIN GAUGE

• One set (5) size 1 (2.25mm) double-pointed needles (dpns)

• One size B/1 (2.25mm) crochet hook

• Stitch markers and scrap yarn

GAUGE
26 sts and 40 rows = 4"/10cm over double knit and charted pattern, after blocking, using size 1 (2.25mm) needles.
TAKE TIME TO CHECK GAUGE.

PROVISIONAL CAST-ON
Using scrap yarn and crochet hook, ch the number of sts to cast on plus a few extra. Cut a tail and

pull the tail through the last chain. With knitting needle and yarn, pick up and knit the stated number of sts through the "purl bumps" on the back of the chain. To remove waste chain, when instructed, pull out the tail from the last crochet stitch. Gently and slowly pull on the tail to unravel the crochet stitches, carefully placing each released knit stitch on a needle.

DOUBLE KNIT

The charted portion of this hat is worked in double knit as foll: with one strand of each color at back, knit the first (RS) st with color indicated on chart. Move both strands to front of work and purl the 2nd (WS) st with the opposite color. These 2 sts are represented by 1 square on the chart. Each set of sts will always contain 1 MC st and 1 CC st.

BRIM

With circular needle and MC, cast-on 136 sts using provisional cast-on. PM and join, being careful not to twist sts. Work in St st (k on RS, p on WS) for 3 rounds.

Next rnd Release the provisional cast-on and distribute these 136 sts evenly over 4 dpns; pm for beg of rnd, taking care that this marker lines up with first marker. With purl side facing, join CC to these new sts and purl 1 rnd.

Setup for double knit pat

With RS facing out, fold CC section of work to inside of MC section. With circular needle, *sl 1 MC, sl 1 CC from dpns; rep from * until all 272 sts are on one circular needle. **Note** From here on, both colors will be used in each round.

Next rnd With MC and CC at back, work in double knit as foll: *k1 MC, move MC and CC to front of work, p1 CC; repeat from * around.

Next rnd [Work 20 sts as established, pm] 7 times, work 14 sts, pm, [work 20 sts, pm] 5 times, work 18 sts.

Beg chart

Work each rnd as foll: A section of chart over 118 sts, B section of chart over 36 sts, rep A section over 118 sts. When 28 rnds of chart are complete, work one rnd even in double knit.

CROWN

Setup rnd *Sl 1 MC, move 1 CC to scrap yarn; rep from * around—136 sts on needle (for outer crown), 136 sts held (for inner crown).

Outer crown

With MC, work in St st (k every rnd) until piece measures 5½"/14cm from beg.

Shape crown

Next rnd *K2tog, k32; rep from * around—132 sts. Knit 1 rnd.

Next rnd *K2tog, k9; rep from * around—120 sts. Knit 1 rnd.

Next rnd *K2tog, k8; rep from * around—108 sts. Knit 1 rnd.

Next rnd *K2tog, k7; rep from * around—96 sts. Knit 1 rnd.

Next rnd *K2tog, k6; rep from * around—84 sts. Knit 1 rnd.

Next rnd *K2tog, k5; rep from * around—72 sts. Knit 1 rnd.

Next rnd *K2tog, k4; rep from * around—60 sts. Knit 1 rnd.

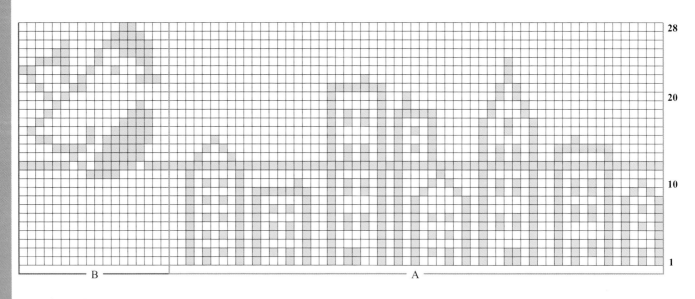

Color Key

☐ wyib, k1 MC, then wyif, p1 CC   ▨ wyib, k1 CC, then wyif, p1 MC

Next rnd *K2tog, k3; rep from * around—48 sts.
Knit 1 rnd.

Next rnd *K2tog, k2; rep from * around—36 sts.
Knit 1 rnd.

Next rnd *K2tog, k1; rep from * around—24 sts.
Knit 1 rnd.

Next rnd *K2tog; rep from * around—12 sts.

Next rnd *K2tog; rep from * around—6 sts.
Cut yarn, thread tail through rem sts and
draw closed. Weave in end.

Inner crown

Move held sts back to circular needle.
With CC, work in St st until inner crown
measures slightly less than 5½"/14cm from beg.
Work same as for outer crown. ∎

Two-Color Geometric Hat

Kyle Kunnecke's beanie features a simple shape with a striking color pattern that would flatter a man or a woman. The pattern is reminiscent of mosaic knitting, but is actually stranded colorwork.

SIZE

Instructions are written for one size.

KNITTED MEASUREMENTS

Circumference approx 22"/56cm
Length approx 7¾"/19.5cm

MATERIALS

• 1 1¾oz/50g hank (each approx 191yd/175m) of Shibui *Staccato* (superwash merino wool/silk/nylon) each in #112 redwood (MC) and #115 chrome (CC) ①

• Contrasting sock-weight yarn (waste yarn)

• One each sizes 1 and 2 (2.25 and 2.75mm) circular needles, 16"/40cm long,
OR SIZE TO OBTAIN GAUGE

• One set (5) size 2 (2.75mm) double-pointed needles (dpns)

• Size C/2 (2.75mm) crochet hook

• Stitch marker

GAUGE

32 sts and 34 rnds = 4"/10cm over chart pat using larger needle.
TAKE TIME TO CHECK GAUGE.

NOTE To work in the rnd, always read chart from right to left.

STITCH GLOSSARY

Joining brim facing

Holding circular needles parallel, insert a dpn knitwise into first st of each needle and wrap yarn around each needle as if to knit. Knit these 2 sts tog and sl them off the needles, *k the next 2 sts tog in the same manner; rep from * around foll chart pat.

HAT

Brim facing

With crochet hook and waste yarn, ch 178 for chain-st provisional cast-on. Cut yarn and draw end through lp on hook. Turn ch so bottom lps are at top and cut end is at left. With smaller circular needle and CC, beg 2 lps from right end, pick up and k 1 st in each of next 176 lps. Join and pm, taking care not to twist sts on needle. Work around in St st (knit every rnd) for 15 rnds.

Next rnd With MC, knit.

Next (turning ridge) rnd With MC, purl.

Next rnd With MC, knit. Change to larger needle.

Beg chart pat

Rnd 1 (RS) Work 16-st rep 11 times. Cont to foll chart in this way through rnd 10.

Joining brim facing

With RS facing, release cut end from lp of waste yarn ch. Pulling out 1 ch at a time, place 176 live sts on smaller circular needle. Bring smaller needle up and behind larger needle, WS tog.

Rnd 11 (joining) Foll instructions for joining brim facing, work 16-st rep 11 times. Cont chart on rnd 12 and work through rnd 34.

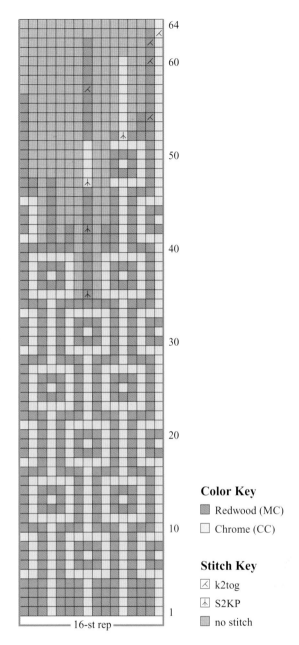

Color Key
- ▨ Redwood (MC)
- ☐ Chrome (CC)

Stitch Key
- ◸ k2tog
- ⟁ S2KP
- ▨ no stitch

16-st rep

Crown shaping

Change to dpns (dividing sts evenly among 4 needles) when there are too few sts on circular needle.

Cont chart on rnd 35 and work through rnd 64—11 sts. Cut CC, leaving a 10"/25.5cm tail, and thread through rem sts twice. Pull tog tightly and secure end. Cut MC and weave in end on WS. ■

Modern Chullo

Pam Allen's contemporary earflap hat features dazzling stranded colorwork, but omits the pompoms and tassels of the traditional Andean hat.

SIZE

Instructions are written for one size.

KNITTED MEASUREMENTS

Circumference approx 21"/53cm

MATERIALS

• 1 1¾oz/50g ball (each approx 114yd/105m) of Koigu Wool Designs *Kersti Merino Crepe* (wool) each in #1014 blue (A), #1520 lime (B), #1515 aqua (C), #1100 red (D), #1150 pink (E), and #1190 orange (F) (3)

• One size 6 (4mm) circular needle, 16"/40cm long, OR SIZE TO OBTAIN GAUGE

• One set (4) size 6 (4mm) double-pointed needles (dpns)

• Size E/4 (3.5mm) crochet hook

• Stitch markers

GAUGE

21 sts and 32 rows = 4"/10cm in St st over charts using size 6 (4mm) circular needle.
TAKE TIME TO CHECK GAUGE.

CHULLO

With A and circular needle, cast on 112 sts. Join, taking care not to twist sts on needle. Place marker for end of rnd and sl marker every rnd. K 3 rnds.
Next 2 rnds *K1 A, k1 B; rep from * around.
With A, k 2 rnds.
Next rnd *K1 E, k1 A; rep from * around. With D, k 1 rnd. With B, k 1 rnd. With A, k 2 rnds. With C, k 1 rnd. Work 11 rnds of chart 1 (working 14-st rep 8 times). With A, k 2 rnds. With B, k 1 rnd. With D, k 1 rnd. With C, k 1 rnd.
Next (dec) rnd With C, k6, *k2tog, k12; rep from *, end last rep k6—104 sts.
Next rnd K1 F, *k5 A, k3 F; rep from *, end k2 F. With C, k 1 rnd. Work 5 rnds of chart 2 (working 8-st rep 13 times). With A, k 1 rnd.
Next (dec) rnd *K1 A, k1 E; rep from *, AT SAME TIME work dec rnd as foll: *ssk, k1, pm, k1, k2tog, k7; rep from *, end k4—88 sts.
Next rnd With D, knit.
Next rnd With C, work to 3 sts before marker, ssk, k2, k2tog, k5; rep from * around—72 sts. Rep last 2 rnds twice—40 sts.
Next (dec) rnd Work to 3 sts between decs, *sl 2 knitwise, k1, psso, k2; rep from * around—24 sts.
Next rnd With A, knit.
Next (dec) rnd With A, *k1, k2tog; rep from * around—16 sts.
Next rnd With A, knit.

Next (dec) rnd *K2tog; rep from * around—8 sts. Cut yarn, leaving 6"/15.5cm tail, and thread through rem sts. Pull tog tightly and secure end.

Earflaps

With hat upside down, RS and center back facing, beg in 18th st to the left of center back, with A, pick up and k 21 sts.

Row 1 (WS) With A, knit. Cont to work back and forth in garter st as foll: K 4 rows A, k 4 rows C.

Next row (RS) *Sl 1, k1 D; rep from *, end sl 1.

Next row *Sl 1, bring yarn to front, k1, bring yarn to back; rep from *, end sl 1.

Next row (RS) *K1 C, sl 1; rep from *, end k1 C. K 2 rows with B. K 4 rows with A.

Eyelet dec row With C, k2, k2tog, yo, ssk, k to last 6 sts, k2tog, yo, ssk, k2—19 sts.

Next row With C, knit. Rep last 2 rows twice—15 sts.

Next 6 rows With A, rep eyelet dec row every RS row 3 times—9 sts.

Next row With A, k2, k2tog, yo, ssk, sl 2 knitwise, k1, psso, k2tog, yo, ssk, k2—7 sts.

Next row Knit.

Last row Ssk, sl 1, k2tog, psso, bind off, k2tog, bind off last st.

Work 2nd earflap opposite first.

FINISHING

With RS facing and crochet hook, beg at center back lower edge of hat, work sc evenly all along lower edge, alternating 1 st A and 1 st C, and substituting D for C along curved edges of each flap. ■

CHART 1

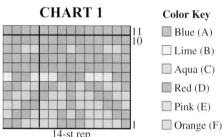

11
10

1

14-st rep

CHART 2

5

1

8-st rep

Color Key

- ■ Blue (A)
- □ Lime (B)
- ▨ Aqua (C)
- ▨ Red (D)
- ▨ Pink (E)
- ▨ Orange (F)

Striped Cloche

Linda Medina's cozy cloche is knit in the round in a striped knot pattern. The subtle mauve and cocoa color palette will take you through the seasons.

SIZE

Instructions are written for one size.

KNITTED MEASUREMENTS

Circumference approx 23"/58.5cm

Length (excluding brim) approx 6½"/16.5cm

MATERIALS

• 2 1¾oz/50g balls (each approx 123yd/113m) of Rowan/Westminster Fibers *Wool Cotton* (cotton/merino wool) each in #977 frozen (MC) and #965 mocha (CC) (3)

• One size 5 (3.75mm) circular needle, 16"/40cm long, OR SIZE TO OBTAIN GAUGE

• One set (5) size 5 (3.75mm) dpns

• Stitch marker

GAUGE

22 sts and 36 rnds = 4"/10cm over stripe pat st using size 5 (3.75mm) needle.
TAKE TIME TO CHECK GAUGE.

STITCH GLOSSARY

kfb Inc 1 by knitting into the front and back of the next st.

STRIPE PATTERN STITCH

(over a multiple of 2 sts plus 1)

Rnd 1 With MC, knit.

Rnd 2 With MC, *k2tog, leaving sts on LH needle, then p same 2 sts tog, sl both sts from needle; rep from * around, end sl 1.

Rnd 3 With CC, knit.

Rnd 4 With CC, k1, *k2tog, leaving sts on LH needle, then p same 2 sts tog, sl both sts from needle; rep from * around.

Rep rnds 1–4 for stripe pat st.

CLOCHE

Brim facing

With circular needle and MC, cast on 127 sts. Join and pm, taking care not to twist sts on needle.

Rnds 1-5 Knit.

Rnd 6 (inc) *K10, kfb; rep from * around to last 6 sts, end k4, kfb, k1—139 sts.

Rnds 7 and 8 Knit.

Rnd 9 (inc) *K2, kfb; rep from * around, end k1—185 sts.

Rnds 10-16 Knit.

Rnd 17 With CC, knit.

Rnd 18 (turning ridge) With CC, purl.

Brim

Rnds 1-12 Rep rnds 1–4 of stripe pat st 3 times.

Rnd 13 (dec) With MC, *k2, k2tog; rep from * around, end k1—139 sts.

Rnd 14 Work rnd 2 of stripe pat st.

Rnd 15 (dec) With CC, *k10, k2tog; rep from * around to last 7 sts, end k2, k2tog, k3—127 sts.

Rnd 16 Work rnd 4 of stripe pat st.

Rnds 17 and 18 Work rnds 1 and 2 of stripe pat st. Cut MC.

Hatband

Next (dec) rnd With CC, k to last 2 sts, end k2tog—126 sts.

Rnds 1-4 *K1, p1; rep from * around.

Rnds 5 and 6 Purl.

Rnds 7-10 *K1, p1; rep from * around.

Crown

Next (inc) rnd With MC, kfb, knit to end—127 sts. Work rnds 2–4 of stripe pat, then rep rnds 1–4 four times, then rnds 1 and 2 once.

Crown shaping

Change to dpns (dividing sts evenly among 4 needles) when there are too few sts on circular needle.

Rnd 1 (dec) With CC, *k13, k2tog; rep from * around to last 7 sts, end k7—119 sts.

Rnd 2 Work rnd 4 of stripe pat st.

Rnds 3-6 Rep rnds 1–4 of stripe pat st.

Rnd 7 (dec) With MC, *k11, k2tog; rep from * around to last 2 sts, end k2—110 sts.

Note Beg with rnd 8, the placement of the sl st changes. Cont to work as foll:

Rnd 8 With MC, *k2tog, leaving sts on LH needle, then p same 2 sts tog, sl both sts from needle; rep from * around.

Rnd 9 Work rnd 3 of stripe pat st.

Rnd 10 With CC, k1, *k2tog, leaving sts on LH needle, then p same 2 sts tog, sl both sts from needle; rep from * around, end sl 1.

Rnd 11 (dec) With MC, *k4, k2tog; rep from * around, end k2—92 sts.

Rnd 12 With MC, *k2tog, leaving sts on LH needle, then p same 2 sts tog, sl both sts from needle; rep from * around.

Rnd 13 (dec) With CC, *k3, k2tog; rep from * around, end k2—74 sts.

Rnd 14 Rep rnd 10.

Rnd 15 (dec) With MC, *k2, k2tog; rep from * around, end k2—56 sts.

Rnd 16 Rep rnd 12.

Rnd 17 (dec) With CC, *k1, k2tog; rep from * around, end k2—38 sts.

Rnd 18 Rep rnd 10.

Rnd 19 (dec) With MC, *k2tog; rep from * around—19 sts.

Rnd 20 Work rnd 2 of stripe pat st.

Rnd 21 (dec) With CC, *k2tog; rep from * around, end k1—10 sts. Cut CC, leaving a 10"/25.5cm tail, and thread through rem sts twice. Pull tog tightly and secure end. Cut MC and weave in end on WS.

FINISHING

Turn brim facing to WS along turning ridge, then whipstitch edge in place using MC. ■

Two-Tone Chullo

Helen Bingham updates the classic Peruvian earflap hat using sophisticated shades of blue-green and chocolate and graphic Fair Isle motifs.

SIZE

Instructions are written for one size.

KNITTED MEASUREMENTS

Circumference approx 20"/51cm
Length (excluding earflaps) approx 8½"/21.5cm

MATERIALS

• 1 3½oz/100g skein (each approx 190yd/174m) of Brown Sheep *Lamb's Pride Worsted* (wool/mohair) each in #M16 seafoam (MC) and #M89 roasted coffee (CC) (4)

• One size 8 (5mm) circular needle, 16"/40cm long, OR SIZE TO OBTAIN GAUGE

• One set (5) size 8 (5mm) double-pointed needles (dpns)

• Size G/6 (4mm) crochet hook

• Stitch marker

GAUGE

22 sts and 24 rnds = 4"/10cm over chart pats using size 8 (5mm) needle. TAKE TIME TO CHECK GAUGE.

NOTES

1) Chart 1 (earflap) is worked back and forth. Always read odd (RS) rows from right to left and even (WS) rows from left to right.
2) To work remaining charts in the rnd, always read charts from right to left.

LEFT EARFLAP

With MC and dpn, cast on 3 sts. Working back and forth in St st (knit on RS, purl on WS) using 2 dpn, cont as foll:

Beg chart pat 1

Row 1 (inc) (RS) K1, [M1, k1] twice—5 sts.

Row 2 P5. Cont to foll chart in this way until row 15 is completed, end with a RS row—19 sts. (Row 16 is worked later.) Cut yarns. Leave sts on dpns.

RIGHT EARFLAP

With MC and circular needle, cast on 3 sts. Working back and forth in St st, cont to work as for left earflap, end with a RS row—19 sts. Do not cut yarns. Leave sts on needle.

CHULLO

With circular needle (holding right earflap sts), MC and CC held tog, and using backward-loop cast-on method, cast on 45 sts (front of hat), work row 16 of chart 1 over 19 sts of left earflap, cast on 29 sts (back of hat), join to work in the rnd, then work row 16 of chart 1 over 19 sts of right earflap—112 sts. Using MC, k2, then pm for beg of rnds.

Beg chart pat 2

Rnd 1 (RS) Work 16-st rep 7 times. Cont to foll chart in this way through rnd 38.

Crown Shaping

Change to dpn (dividing sts evenly among 4 needles) when there are too few sts on circular needle.

Beg chart pat 3

Rnd 1 (dec) (RS) Work 16-st rep 7 times—84 sts. Work rnd 2.

Rnd 3 (dec) Work 12-st rep 7 times—56 sts. Work rnd 4. Cut MC and cont with CC only as foll:

Rnd 5 (dec) [Ssk] 28 times—28 sts.

Rnd 6 Knit.

Rnd 7 (dec) [Ssk] 14 times—14 sts.

Rnd 8 Knit.

Rnd 9 [Ssk] 7 times—7 sts. Cut CC, leaving an 8"/20.5cm tail, and thread through rem sts. Pull tog tightly and secure end.

FINISHING

Steam lightly to even out stitches.

Edging

With RS facing, crochet hook and CC, join yarn with a sl st in center back edge. **Rnd 1 (RS)** Ch 1, making sure that work lies flat, sc evenly around entire edge, join rnd with a sl st in first sc. **Rnd 2 (RS)** Do not ch, sl st in each st around, join rnd with a sl st in first sl st. Fasten off.

Braids

For each braid, cut three 50"/127cm-long strands each of MC and CC. Place strands together, then fold in half. Working from WS to RS, insert crochet hook through first row of sc at center bottom of left earflap. Use hook to draw folded end of strands through, forming a loop, then use hook to draw strands through loop. Gently pull on strands to snug up loop. Divide strands into 3 groups of 4 strands. Braid to within 6"/15cm of ends. Make a firm overhand knot at base of braid forming a tassel. Trim ends evenly if necessary. Rep for right earflap. ■

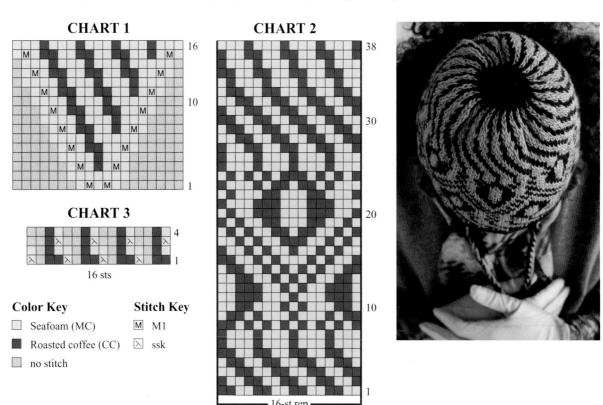

CHART 1

CHART 3

16 sts

CHART 2

16-st rep

Color Key

☐ Seafoam (MC)

■ Roasted coffee (CC)

▨ no stitch

Stitch Key

Ⓜ M1

⊠ ssk

Brioche Swirl Hat

Nancy Marchant's slouchy hat has a deep, folded brim. The brioche stitch is worked in a swirl pattern and is reversible—two hats for the price of one!

Light side of reversible hat.

SIZE

Instructions are written for one size.

KNITTED MEASUREMENTS

Circumference (slightly stretched) approx 22"/56cm
Length (with cuff folded up) approx 11½"/29cm

MATERIALS

• 1 1¾oz/50g ball (each approx 195yd/180m) of Crystal Palace *Mini Mochi* (merino wool/nylon) each in #312 seafoam (LC) and #124 leaves & sprout (DC) (2)

• One size 4 (3.5mm) circular needle, 16"/40cm long, OR SIZE TO OBTAIN GAUGE

• One set (4) size 4 (3.5mm) double-pointed needles (dpns)

• Stitch marker

GAUGE

16 sts and 24 rnds = 4"/10cm over swirl brioche st using size 4 (3.5mm) needle. TAKE TIME TO CHECK GAUGE.

NOTES

1) Hat is made from the top down.
2) Brioche knitting creates a cushy reversible ribbed fabric. This comes about by working one stitch and slipping the next. In brioche knitting, instead of carrying the working yarn in front or in back of the slipped stitch, you bring the yarn over the stitch, giving the stitch a little shawl over its

shoulders. In the following round, this shawled stitch will be either barked or burped (refer to stitch glossary).

3) Each round is worked twice; half of the stitches are worked with DC in one round and the other half (the stitches that were slipped in the former round) are worked in the following round with LC. You should count the DC knit column sts for the correct number of rounds worked.

4) Don't cross your threads when changing colors at the end/beginning of a round. At the end of a DC round, your last stitch will be a sl1yo; bring the DC thread to the front after working the stitch and let it hang there. Pick up the LC from under the DC thread and work the first stitch of the LC round, which is also a sl1yo.

5) The last stitch at the end of a LC round will be a "burp" stitch. Since the DC is hanging to the front you should be able to maintain the DC yo to work this last "burp" stitch with LC. Then keep the LC thread in front, pick up DC, and without crossing the threads, take it to the back to work the first stitch of the next round, which will be a brk1.

6) Increases and decreases: To maintain the patterning of brioche stitches, increases and decreases should be worked in pairs. After working an increase in a DC round, three DC stitches bloom out of the center of one stitch. These 3 scrunched-together stitches will be worked separately in the following LC round as "sl1yo, p1, sl1yo."

7) If at some point you need to "frog," then unravel and pick up the stitches onto a smaller circular needle. This will make the stitches easier to pick up and you can work off of this needle, onto your original needle, for one round.

STITCH GLOSSARY

DC (dark color) Work with dark color yarn.

LC (light color) Work with light color yarn.

brk (brioche knit; also known as a bark) Knit the stitch (that was slipped in the rnd before) together with its yarn over.

brkyobrk (bark 1, yarn over, bark 1) 2-stitch increase; brk1, leaving st on LH needle, yo (yarn forward under needle, then over needle to back), then brk1 into same stitch—2 stitches inc.

brp (brioche purl; also known as a burp) Purl the stitch (that was slipped in the rnd before) together with its yarn over.

brRsl dec (brioche right slant decrease) 2-stitch decrease that slants to the right, involves 3 sts; slip the first stitch kwise, knit the next stitch, pass the slipped stitch over, place live stitch on LH needle, and pass the following stitch over. Place live st on RH needle.

k1yok1 (knit 1, yarn over, knit 1) 2-stitch increase; knit 1, yarn over (yarn forward under needle, then over needle to back), then knit 1 into same stitch.

sl1yo This action creates the shawled stitch. It works differently for a bark round than for a burp round, but one manipulation remains standard—that the working yarn must always be in front before slipping the stitch. On a burp round, the working yarn is already in front before slipping the stitch, but in a bark round you need to first bring the yarn to the front and then slip the stitch. This worked stitch with its yarn-over shawl is considered one stitch.

sl1yo (following a k or brk st) Bring the working yarn under the needle to the front of the work, slip the next stitch purlwise, then bring the yarn over the needle (and over the slipped stitch) to the back, in position to work the following stitch.

sl1yo (following a p or brp st) Working yarn is already in front; slip the next stitch purlwise, then bring the yarn over the needle (and over the slipped stitch), then to the front under the needle, into position to work the following stitch.

HAT

Beg at center top of hat, with dpn and LC, cast on 4 sts using backward loop method. Work short I-cord nub as foll: ***Next row (RS)** With 2nd dpn, k4, do not turn. Slide sts back to beg of needle to work next row from RS; rep from * twice more.
Setup rnd LC [K1yok1] 4 times—12 sts. Do not turn; slide sts back to beg of needle to work next row from RS. Join DC.
Rnd 1 DC With DC, *k1, sl1yo; rep from * to end— remember that a st and its yo are considered one st, so you will still have 12 sts. You are now going to work in the round, so divide sts onto 3 dpns (4 sts on first needle, 4 sts on second needle, and 4 sts on third needle). Bury yarn tails in I-cord nub to keep them out of the way.
Rnd 1 LC Keep DC in front to maintain yo of last worked st; with LC, *sl1yo, brp1; rep from *around.
Rnd 2 DC [Brkyobrk, sl1yo] 6 times—24 sts (12 sts inc).
Rnd 2 LC [Sl1yo, p1, sl1yo, brp1] 6 times. Pm on first st to indicate beg of rnd. This hat is divided into six sections; each section begins where the rep begins. After a few more rounds, place a marker before the first DC st at beg of the other 5 sections.

Rnd 3 DC *Brk1, sl1yo; rep from * around—24 sts (4 sts per section).
Rnd 3 LC *Sl1yo, brp1; rep from * around—24 sts.
Rnd 4 DC *Brkyobrk, sl1yo, brk1, sl1yo; rep from * around—36 sts.
Rnd 4 LC *Sl1yo, p1, [sl1yo, brp1] twice; rep from * around.
Rnds 5 DC and LC Rep rnds 3 DC and LC.
Rnd 6 DC *Brkyobrk, sl1yo, [brk1, sl1yo] twice; rep from * around—48 sts.
Rnd 6 LC *Sl1yo, p1, [sl1yo, brp1] 3 times; rep from * around.
Rnds 7 and 8 DC and LC Rep rnds 3 DC and LC.
Rnd 9 DC *Brkyobrk, sl1yo, [brk1, sl1yo] 3 times; rep from * around—60 sts.
Rnd 9 LC *Sl1yo, p1, [sl1yo, brp1] 4 times; rep from * around.
Rnds 10 DC and LC Rep rnds 3 DC and LC.
Rnds 11 DC and LC Rep rnds 3 DC and LC.
Rnd 12 DC *Brkyobrk, sl1yo, [brk1, sl1yo] 4 times; rep from * around—72 sts.
Rnd 12 LC *Sl1yo, p1, [sl1yo, brp1] 5 times; rep from * around.
Rnds 13 DC and LC Rep rnds 3 DC and LC.
Rnds 14 DC and LC Rep rnds 3 DC and LC.
Rnd 15 DC *Brkyobrk, sl1yo, [brk1, sl1yo] 5 times; rep from * around—84 sts.
Rnd 15 LC *Sl1yo, p1, [sl1yo, brp1] 6 times; rep from * around.
Rnds 16 DC and LC Rep rnds 3 DC and LC.
Rnds 17 DC and LC Rep rnds 3 DC and LC.
Rnds 18 DC and LC Rep rnds 3 DC and LC.
Rnd 19 DC *Brkyobrk, sl1yo, [brk1, sl1yo] 6 times; rep from * around—96 sts.
Rnd 19 LC *Sl1yo, p1, [sl1yo, brp1] 7 times; rep from * around.

Light side (left), dark side (above).

Rnds 20 DC and LC Rep rnds 3 DC and LC.

Rnds 21 DC and LC Rep rnds 3 DC and LC.

Rnds 22 DC and LC Rep rnds 3 DC and LC.

Rnd 23 DC *Brkyobrk, sl1yo, [brk1, sl1yo] 7 times; rep from * around—108 sts.

Rnd 23 LC *Sl1yo, p1, [sl1yo, brp1] 8 times; rep from * around.

Rnds 24 DC and LC Rep rnd 3 DC and LC.

Rnds 25 DC and LC Rep rnd 3 DC and LC.

Rnds 26 DC and LC Rep rnd 3 DC and LC. Beg brioche swirl st as foll:

Rnd 27 DC *Brkyobrk, sl1yo, [brk1, sl1yo] 6 times, brRsl dec, sl1yo; rep from * around.

Rnd 27 LC *Sl1yo, p1, [sl1yo, brp1] 8 times; rep from * around.

Rnds 28 DC and LC Rep rnds 3 DC and LC.

Rnds 29 DC and LC Rep rnds 3 DC and LC.

Rnds 30 DC and LC Rep rnds 3 DC and LC. Rep rnds 27–30 DC and LC 8 times more or until piece measures 9"/23cm from bottom edge of nub.

Cuff

Rnd 65 LC *Brk1, p1; rep from * around.

Rnd 66 LC *K1, p1; rep from * around. Rep rnd 66 for 5½"/14cm. Bind off loosely. ∎

139

Traveling Vines Beret

The unusual patterning in Lorilee Beltman's colorful beret is accomplished by mixing contrasting purled stranding with increases and decreases to move the purled "vines" around.

SIZE

Instructions are written for one size.

FINISHED MEASUREMENTS

Head circumference 24"/61cm

Brim circumference 19"/48cm

Length 9½"/24cm

MATERIALS

• 3 1¾ oz/50g balls (each approx 100yd/120m) of Noro *Silk Garden Lite* (silk/kid mohair/lambswool) in #2056 purple/pink/green/cocoa 2

• Size 3 (3.25mm) circular needle, 16"/40cm long, OR SIZE TO OBTAIN GAUGE

• One set (5) size 3 (3.25mm) double-pointed needles (dpns)

• Stitch markers

GAUGE

24 sts and 34 rnds = 4"/10cm over St st using size 3 (3.25mm) needles.

TAKE TIME TO CHECK YOUR GAUGE.

STITCH GLOSSARY

RLI (right lifted inc) Insert RH needle from back to front into RH leg of st 1 row below next st on LH needle and place loop on LH needle, k this st.

LLI (left lifted inc) Insert LH needle from back to front into LH leg of st 2 rnds below st just worked on RH needle and k into the back of it.

TWISTED RIB

(over an even number of sts)

Rnd 1 K1 by inserting RH needle in next st as if to knit and wrapping yarn clockwise over the top of the RH needle to twist the st, p1; rep from * to end. Rep rnd 1 for twisted rib.

NOTES

1) Hat is worked from top to lower edge in the rnd. Strands of contrasting colors (CC) are cut from a separate ball of yarn and added in as the chart is worked.

2) To keep contrasting colors from tangling as you work, thread beg tails to RS of work after 1 rnd has been worked. Then, untangle working ends of contrasting strands and, holding the 6 strands tog, wind around finger and thumb in figure 8 to form a butterfly, tying center tightly with a separate strand of yarn. Keep butterfly hanging at WS of work. When rnd 13 is complete and 6 additional strands have been added, re-form butterfly using 12 strands.

3) Pick up CC from under main yarn to prevent holes in work, and pull working CC strand firmly to tighten st in previous rnd.

SETUP

Cut 12 strands, each approx 2yd/2m long, of contrasting colors from one ball of yarn. 6 separate strands are added in each of chart rnds 1 and 13.

BERET

With full ball of yarn (MC), cast on 4 sts, leaving a 12"/30.5cm tail. Join, taking care not to twist sts, and place marker (pm) for beg of rnd.

Next rnd Holding tail and working yarn tog, k4. Drop tail.

Next (inc) rnd With working yarn, k 1 rnd, separating each doubled st into 2 single sts—8 sts. Knit 1 rnd.

Next (inc) rnd [K1, LLI, RLI, k1] 4 times—16 sts. Knit 2 rnds.

Next (inc) rnd [K1, LLI, RLI, k1, pm] 8 times—32 sts. K 3 rnds.

Next (inc) rnd [K2, LLI, RLI, k2, sl marker] 8 times—48 sts.

Cont to inc in this manner every 4th rnd, working 1 more st at beg and end of each marked section, 6 times more—18 sts in each marked section, 144 sts in rnd.

Knit 1 rnd, removing all but the beg of rnd marker.

Beg chart

Note When adding new strand of CC, l eave a tail 6–8"/15–20.5cm long.

Rnd 1 K3, work 18-st rep 3 times, k to end of rnd. Cont to foll chart in this manner until rnd 21 is complete.

Next (dec) rnd Work in pat, k the knit sts and p the purl sts in CC, over next 20 sts, k2tog, work next 17 sts in pat, k2tog, work in pat to end of rnd—142 sts.

Next rnd Work even in pat.

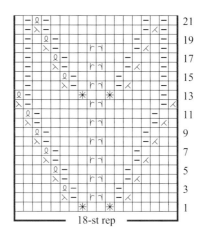

18-st rep

Stitch Key

☐ k
⊟ p in CC
⊠ k2tog
⊠ ssk
⊠ k1tbl
⊡ LLI
⊡ RLI
✳ k1 in new strand of CC

Next (dec) rnd K2, k2tog, work next 7 sts in pat, k2tog, [work next 15 sts in pat, k2tog] twice, work next 7 sts in pat, *k2tog, k7; rep from * to last 7 sts, k2tog, k5—128 sts.

Beg twisted rib pat

Foll twisted rib pat, purling sts in CC as they appear, until piece measures 10"/25.5cm.

Last rnd Work next 92 sts in pat, bind off in MC only as foll: Yo from back to front, k1, pass yo over k st, *yo from back to front, k1, insert LH needle under yo and previously worked st, pass over k st; rep from * until 1 st rem, break yarn and pull through rem st.

FINISHING

Weave beg tails of CC to WS of hat. Weave each CC strand into column of k sts on WS to enhance the bulk of the purled line of sts. ■

Fair Isle Fez

Mary Ann Stephens's regal fez is knit in the round and features a graphic stranded colorwork pattern. A frisky tassel keeps it from being too serious.

SIZE

Instructions are written for one size.

KNITTED MEASUREMENTS

Circumference 20"/51cm
Length 9"/23cm

MATERIALS

• One 1¾/50g hank (each approx 164yd/150m) of Cascade Yarns *Cascade 220 Sport* (wool) each in #8555 black (MC) and #8505 white (CC) (3)

• One each sizes 4 and 6 (3.5 and 4mm) circular needles, 16"/40cm long style, OR SIZE TO OBTAIN GAUGE

• One set (5) size 6 (4mm) double-pointed needles (dpns)

• 2 size 4 (3.5mm) dpns for I-cord

• Stitch markers

GAUGES

24 sts and 32 rows = 4"/10cm over St st using size 6 (4mm) needles, after blocking.
24 sts and 28 rows = 4"/10cm over colorwork using size 6 (4mm) needles, after blocking.
TAKE TIME TO CHECK GAUGES.

NOTE

When working 2-color rnds, carry the color not in use loosely behind work.

STITCH GLOSSARY

S2KP Sl 2 sts tog knitwise, k1, pass 2 sl sts over the k st—2 sts dec'd.

FEZ

With smaller circular needle and MC, cast on 120 sts. Place marker (pm) for beg of rnd and join, being careful not to twist sts. Beg with a purl rnd, work 10 rnds in garter stitch (k 1 rnd, p 1 rnd). Change to larger needles.

Next rnd *K1 CC, k1 MC; rep from * around.

Next rnd *P1 CC, k1 MC; rep from * around.

K 1 rnd MC. K 1 rnd CC. K 1 rnd MC.

Beg chart

Rnd 1 Work the 30 st rep 4 times around. Cont to work chart in this manner through rnd 32.

Crown shaping

Note Change to dpns when sts no longer fit comfortably on circular needle.

Rnd 33 Work in chart pat to 1 st before marker.

Rnd 34 (dec) Sl last st of rnd 33, remove marker, place slipped st back on LH needle, pm on RH needle for beg of rnd, S2KP, work chart rnd 34 to end—112 sts.

Cont to foll chart and work decs as noted on chart in this manner, until rnd 44 is complete—72 sts. Cont to foll chart and work dec rnd every rnd as noted on chart through rnd 53—8 sts.

Remove marker. Cut MC. With CC, [k2tog] 5 times—3 sts.

I-cord

With smaller dpns and CC, make I-cord as foll: *K3, do not turn work; slide sts to opposite end of

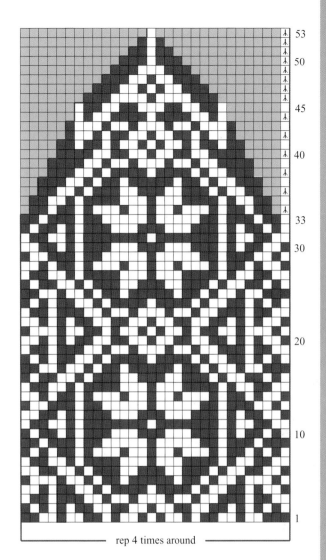

rep 4 times around

Color Key
- ■ Black (MC)
- □ White (CC)

Stitch Key
- ⟂ S2KP with CC
- ▨ no stitch

needle, bring yarn across back of work to work next row from the RS; rep from * until I-cord is approx 6"/15cm long. K3tog and fasten off, leaving a tail 4"/10cm long.

FINISHING

Tassel

With MC and CC held tog, make 2½"/6.5cm tassel. Attach tassel to I-cord. Block cap if necessary, avoiding lower edges. ■

COLOR

145

Chevron Hat

Brenda Castiel uses multicolored yarn for stripes with minimal effort.

SIZE

Instructions are written for one size.

KNITTED MEASUREMENTS

Circumference approx 22½"/57cm

Length approx 8"/20.5cm

MATERIALS

• 1 1¾oz/50g skein (approx 110yd/100m) of Noro/KFI *Silk Garden* (silk/mohair/lambswool) in #258 (4)

• One size 7 (4.5mm) circular needle, 16"/40cm long, OR SIZE TO OBTAIN GAUGE

• One set (5) size 7 (4.5mm) dpns

• Stitch markers

GAUGE

17 sts and 24 rnds = 4"/10cm over chevron pat using size 7 (4.5mm) needle.

STITCH GLOSSARY

kfb Inc 1 by knitting into front and back of next st.

CHEVRON PATTERN (over a multiple of 12 sts)

Rnd 1 *K2tog, k3, [kfb] twice, k3, ssk; rep from * around. **Rnd 2** Knit. Rep rnds 1 and 2 for chevron pat.

HAT

With circular needle, cast on 90 sts. Join and pm, taking care not to twist sts on needle. Cont in garter st (k one rnd, purl one rnd) for 4 rnds. **Next (inc) rnd** *K14, kfb; rep from * around—96 sts. Rep rnds 1 and 2 of chevron pat 3 times, then rnd 1 once.

Next (garter ridge) rnd Purl. Rep rnds 1 and 2 of chevron pat 4 times, then rnd 1 once. **Next (garter ridge) rnd** Purl. Cont in chevron pat until piece measures 5"/12.5cm from beg (measuring from bottom edge of point), end with rnd 2.

Crown shaping

Change to dpns (dividing sts evenly among 4 needles) when there are too few sts on circular needle. **Rnd 1** *Pm, k2tog, k3,[kfb] twice, k3, ssk; rep from * around—8 markers (including beg of rnd marker). **Rnd 2 (dec)** K2tog, *k to next marker, slip marker, k to 2 sts before next marker, ssk, slip marker, k2tog; rep from * around, end ssk—88 sts. **Rnd 3** *K2tog, k2, [kfb] twice, k3, ssk, k2tog, k3, [kfb] twice, k2, ssk; rep from * around. **Rnd 4 (dec)** *K to 2 sts before next marker, ssk, slip marker, k2tog, k to next marker, slip marker; rep from * around, k to end—80 sts. **Rnd 5** *K2tog, k2, [kfb] twice, k2, ssk; rep from * around. **Rnd 6 (dec)** Rep rnd 2—72 sts. **Rnd 7** *K2tog, k1, [kfb] twice, k2, ssk, k2tog, k2, [kfb] twice, k1, ssk; rep from * around. **Rnd 8 (dec)** Rep rnd 4—64 sts. **Rnd 9** *K2tog, k1, [kfb] twice, k1, ssk; rep from * around. **Rnd 10 (dec)** Rep rnd 2—56 sts. **Rnd 11** *K2tog, [kfb] twice, k1, ssk, k2tog, k1, [kfb] twice, ssk; rep from * around. **Rnd 12 (dec)** Rep rnd 4—48 sts. **Rnd 13** *K2tog, [kfb] twice, ssk; rep from * around. **Rnd 14 (dec)** Rep rnd 2—40 sts. **Rnd 15 (dec)** Rep rnd 4—32 sts. **Rnd 16 (dec)** Rep rnd 2—24 sts. **Rnd 17 (dec)** Rep rnd 4—16 sts. **Rnd 18 (dec)** Rep rnd 2—8 sts. Cut yarn, leaving an 8"/20.5cm tail, and thread through rem sts twice. Pull tog tightly and secure end. ■

Ridged Beret

The subtle stripes in Cathy Carron's jaunty beret come from working two-color stockinette stitch and reverse stockinette stitch ridges.

SIZE

Instructions are written for size Small/Medium (Medium/Large); shown in size Small/Medium.

KNITTED MEASUREMENTS

Circumference 20 (21¾)"/51 (55)cm

MATERIALS

• 1 (1) 3½ oz/100g skein (each approx 436yd/399m) of Misti Alpaca *Tonos Carnaval* (superfine alpaca/merino wool/silk/nylon) each in #TF07 blackberry and #TF05 sand dune (■1)

Note Yarn used in original pattern is no longer available. Original yarn is listed on page 175.

• One size 4 (3.5mm) circular needle, 16"/40cm long, OR SIZE TO OBTAIN GAUGE

• One set (5) size 4 (3.5mm) double-pointed needles (dpns)

• Stitch marker

GAUGE

24 sts and 32 rows = 4"/10cm over St st in the round.
TAKE TIME TO CHECK GAUGE.

BERET

Crown

With A and dpns, cast on 12 sts. Place marker and join for knitting in the round.

Rnd 1 Knit.

Rnd 2 *Knit into front and back of st (kfb); rep from * around—24 sts.

Rnd 3 Knit. Change to B.

Rnds 4-6 Purl. Change to A.

Rnd 7 Knit.

Rnd 8 *K1, kfb; rep from * around—36 sts.

Rnd 9 Knit. **Change to B.

Rnds 10-12 Purl. Change to A.

Rnd 13 Knit.

Rnd 14 *K2, kfb; rep from * around—48 sts.

Rnd 15 Knit. Rep from **, working one more k st before the kfb on each rep, until there are 12 (13) sts before the kfb—168 (180) sts.

Rise

Change to B.

Rnds 1-3 Purl. Change to A.

Rnds 4-5 Knit.

Rnd 6 *K12 (13), k2tog; rep from * around—156 (168) sts.

Rnds 7-11 Rep rnds 1–5.

Rnd 12 *K11(12), k2tog; rep from * around—144 (156) sts.

Rnds 13-17 Rep rnds 1–5.

Rnd 18 *K4, k2tog; rep from * around—120 (130) sts.

FINISHING

With A, knit for 2½"/6.5cm. Bind off loosely. ■

Flower Appliqué Cloche

Elena Malo's simply chic cloche is beautifully embellished with a knit flower. The petals are worked separately and attached to form the flower shape.

KNITTED MEASUREMENTS

Circumference approx 21"/53.5cm

Length approx 8"/20.5cm

MATERIALS

• 2 1¾oz/50g balls (each approx 110yd/100m) of Louisa Harding/KFI *Grace Wool & Silk* (merino wool/silk) in #26 conifer (MC) (3)

• 1 ball in #22 reflection (CC)

• One pair size 6 (4mm) needles OR SIZE TO OBTAIN GAUGE

GAUGE

28 sts = 5"/12.5cm and 32 rows = 4"/10cm over St st using size 6 (4mm) needles. TAKE TIME TO CHECK GAUGE.

STITCH GLOSSARY

kfb Inc 1 by knitting into the front and back of the next st.

kbf Inc 1 by knitting into the back and front of the next st.

CLOCHE

Cuff

With MC, cast on 120 sts.

Rows 1 and 3 Knit.

Rows 2 and 4 Purl. Beg with a purl row, cont in reverse St st (purl on RS, knit on WS) until piece measures 2½"/6.5cm from beg, end with a WS row.

Rise

Cont in St st (knit on RS, purl on WS) until piece measures 7½"/19cm from beg, end with a WS row.

Back shaping

Dec row (RS) K8, ssk, knit to last 10 sts, k2tog, k8. Purl next row. Rep last 2 rows 4 times more—110 sts.

Crown shaping

Dec row 1 (RS) K8, [ssk, k8] 5 times, k2, [k2tog, k8] 5 times—100 sts. Purl next row.

Dec row 2 (RS) K8, [ssk, k7] 5 times, k1, [k2tog, k7] 5 times, end k1—90 sts. Purl next row.

Dec row 3 (RS) K8, [ssk, k6] 5 times, [k2tog, k6] 5 times, end k2—80 sts. Purl next row.

Dec row 4 (RS) K1, [ssk, k5] 5 times, ssk, k4, [k2tog, k5] 5 times, end k2tog, k1—68 sts. Purl next row.

Dec row 5 (RS) K1, [ssk, k4] 5 times, ssk, k2, [k2tog, k4] 5 times, end k2tog, k1—56 sts. Purl next row.

Dec row 6 (RS) K1, [ssk, k3] 5 times, ssk, [k2tog, k3] 5 times, end k2tog, k1—44 sts. Purl next row.

Dec row 7 (RS) K1, [ssk, k2] 5 times, [k2tog, k2] 5 times, end k2tog, k1—33 sts. Purl next row.

Dec row 8 (RS) K1, [ssk, k1] 4 times, ssk, k3tog, [k2tog, k1] 5 times—21 sts. Purl next row.

Dec row 9 (RS) K1, [ssk] 4 times, k3tog, [k2tog] 4 times, k1—11 sts. Cut yarn, leaving a 20"/51cm tail, and thread through rem sts. Pull tog tightly and secure end, then sew back seam, reversing seam over last 3½"/9cm.

FLOWER

Petals (make 10)

With CC, cast on 2 sts.

Row 1 (WS) Purl.

Row 2 (inc) (RS) Kfb, kbf—4 sts.

Row 3 and all odd rows to row 25 Purl.

Row 4 (inc) K1, kfb, kbf, k1—6 sts.

Row 6 (inc) K1, kfb, knit to last 2 sts, kbf, k1—8 sts.

Rows 8, 10, 12, and 14 (inc) Rep row 6—16 sts.

Row 16 Knit.

Row 18 (dec) (RS) Ssk, k4, k2tog, ssk, k4, k2tog—12 sts.

Row 20 (dec) Ssk, k2, k2tog, ssk, k2, k2tog—8 sts.

Row 22 (dec) [Ssk, k2tog] twice—4 sts.

Row 24 (dec) Ssk, k2tog—2 sts.

Row 25 (WS) P2tog. Fasten off last st, leaving one long tail for sewing.

FINISHING

To form cuff, fold up bottom edge 2¾"/7cm to RS; pin in place. Using running stitches, sew in place, just below row 3, forming a decorative raised edge. Lightly steam-press.

Flower

For each petal, fold in half, then sew open edges together using tail. Measure and mark center of RH side of hat, then pinmark ¾"/2cm above decorative raised edge to indicate center of flower. To form flower, work around pinmark and pin bottom edge of each petal in place, making sure that sewn edge is facing down. Using CC, tack sewn edge of each petal to hat, approx 1½"/4cm from tip of petal. ■

Woven Ribbon Cloche

Cheryl Murray's clever cloche features a cable band that wraps around the circumference. Satin ribbon weaves through the cables and forms an accent rosette that takes the topper from everyday to dress-up ready.

SIZES

Instructions are written for size Small (Medium, Large); shown in size Small.

KNITTED MEASUREMENTS

Circumference approx
19 (20¾, 22½)"/48 (52.5, 57)cm
Length (excluding brim) approx
7 ½ (7 ¾, 8)"/19 (19.5, 20.5)cm

MATERIALS

• 1 (2, 2) 3½oz/100g hank (each approx 215yd/198m) Berroco *Ultra Alpaca* (alpaca/wool) in #6219 iris (4)

• Contrasting worsted-weight yarn (waste yarn)

• One each sizes 6 and 7 (4 and 4.5mm) circular needles, 16"/40cm long, OR SIZES TO OBTAIN GAUGE

• One set (5) size 7 (4.5mm) double-pointed needles (dpns)

• Cable needle (cn)

• Size H/8 (5mm) crochet hook

• Stitch marker

• 2 (2¼, 2½)yd/2 (2, 2.25)m of 1"/25mm-wide double-sided satin ribbon in light purple

• Sewing needle and matching sewing thread

• One ⁷⁄₁₆"/11mm button

GAUGE

20 sts and 30 rnds = 4"/10cm over St st using larger needle.
TAKE TIME TO CHECK GAUGE.

NOTES

1) Cabled hatband is worked first.
2) Top of cloche is picked up along one side edge of hatband, then worked to top of crown.
3) Brim of cloche is picked up along opposite side edge of hatband, then worked to top edge of brim facing.

STITCH GLOSSARY

8-st RC Sl 4 sts to cn and hold to back, k4, k4 from cn.
8-st LC Sl 4 sts to cn and hold to front, k4, k4 from cn.

CABLE RIB PATTERN

(over a panel of 21 sts)
Row 1 (RS) K1, p1, k8, p1, k8, p1, k1.
Row 2 P1, k1, p8, k1, p8, k1, p1.
Row 3 K1, p1, 8-st RC, p1, 8-st LC, p1, k1.
Rows 4 and 6 Rep row 2.
Rows 5 and 7 Rep row 1.
Row 8 Rep row 2.
Rep rows 1–8 for cable pat.

CLOCHE

Hatband

With crochet hook and waste yarn, ch 24 for chain-st provisional cast-on. Cut yarn and draw end though lp on hook. Turn ch so bottom lps are at top and cut end is at left. With dpn, beg 2 lps from right end, pick up and k 1 st in each of next 21 lps. Working back and forth on 2 dpns, cont in

cable pat and work even until piece measures approx 20 (21¾, 23½)"/51 (55, 59.5)cm from beg, end with row 6. With RS facing, release cut end from lp of waste yarn ch. Pulling out 1 ch at a time, place 21 live sts on dpn. Join first row to last row, using 3-needle bind-off.

Rise

With RS facing and larger circular needle, pick up and k 96 (104, 112) sts evenly spaced around RH edge of hatband. Join and pm for beg of rnds. Cont in St st (knit every rnd) for 3¼"/8cm.

Crown shaping

Change to dpns (dividing sts evenly among 4 needles) when there are too few sts on circular needle.
Dec rnd 1 *K 10 (11, 12), k2tog; rep from * around—88 (96, 104) sts. Knit next rnd.
Dec rnd 2 *K 9 (10, 11), k2tog; rep from * around—80 (88, 96) sts. Knit next rnd.
Dec rnd 3 *K 8 (9, 10), k2tog; rep from * around—72 (80, 88) sts. Knit next rnd.
Dec rnd 4 *K 7 (8, 9), k2tog; rep from * around—64 (72, 80) sts. Knit next rnd.
Dec rnd 5 *K 6 (7, 8), k2tog; rep from * around—56 (64, 72) sts. Knit next rnd.
Dec rnd 6 *K 5 (6, 7), k2tog; rep from * around—48 (56, 64) sts. Knit next rnd.
Dec rnd 7 *K 4 (5, 6), k2tog; rep from * around—40 (48, 56) sts. Knit next rnd.
Dec rnd 8 *K 3 (4, 5), k2tog; rep from * around—32 (40, 48) sts. Knit next rnd.

For sizes Medium and Large only

Next (dec) rnd *K 3 (4), k2tog; rep from *
around—32 (40) sts. Knit next rnd.

For size Large only

Next (dec) rnd *K3, k2tog; rep from *
around—32 sts. Knit next rnd.

For all sizes

Dec rnd 9 *K2, k2tog; rep from * around—24 sts.
Dec rnd 10 *K1, k2tog; rep from * around—16 sts.
Dec rnd 11 [K2tog] 8 times—8 sts. Cut yarn, leaving
an 8"/20.5cm tail, and thread through rem sts
twice. Pull tog tightly and secure end.

Brim

With RS facing and smaller circular needle, pick
up and k 96 (104, 112) sts evenly spaced around
LH edge of hatband. Join and pm for beg of rnds.
Cont in St st for 4 rnds. Change to larger needle.

For sizes Small and Large only

Next (inc) rnd *K 6 (7), M1; rep from *
around—112 (128) sts.

For size Medium only

Next (inc) rnd *K6, M1, k7, M1;
rep from * around—120 sts.

For all sizes

Work even on 112 (120, 128) sts for 4 rnds.
Next (picot) rnd *Yo, p2tog; rep from * around. Knit
1 rnd. Change to smaller needle.

Brim facing

Knit next 2 rnds.

For sizes Small and Large only

Next (dec) rnd *K 5 (6), k2tog;
rep from * around—96 (112) sts.

For size Medium only

Next (dec) rnd *K5, k2tog, k6, k2tog; rep from *
around—104 sts.

For all sizes

Work even on 96 (104, 112) sts for 5 rnds. Bind
off all sts loosely knitwise.

FINISHING

Fold brim facing to WS along picot rnd and
sew in place.

Ribbon rosette

Cut an 8"/20.5cm-length ribbon. Fold in half,
then sew cut edges together using a ¼"/.5cm seam.
Steam-press seam open. Using thread doubled,
sew small running sts along one edge of ribbon.
Pull thread to gather in center. Fasten off securely.
Set rosette aside. Cut remaining ribbon in half.
Beginning and ending on WS, weave each length
of ribbon through cable twists, taking care to
maintain row gauge and that hatband still has
some stretch. Trim ribbon so ends overlap
by 1"/2.5cm. Sew each pair of ribbon ends tog.
Sew rosette to hatband, placing it over where
ribbon weaving began and ended. Sew button to
center of rosette. ■

Pompom Hat

You'll be ready to hit the slopes after knitting this cozy cabled number. The oversized pompom tops it off perfectly.

SIZE

Instructions are written for one size.

KNITTED MEASUREMENTS

Head circumference 16"/40.5cm (unstretched)
Depth 8"/20.5cm

MATERIALS

• 2 3½oz/100g hanks (each approx 130yd/120m) of Berroco *Vintage Chunky* (wool/acrylic/nylon) in #6114 aster (5)

• One pair size 10½ (6.5mm) needles OR SIZE TO OBTAIN GAUGE

• Cable needle (cn)

GAUGE

12 sts and 22 rows = 4"/10cm over seed st using size 10½ (6.5mm) needles.
TAKE TIME TO CHECK GAUGE.

SEED STITCH

Row 1 (RS) *P1, k1; rep from * to end.
Row 2 K the purl sts and p the knit sts.
Rep row 2 for seed st.

STITCH GLOSSARY

2-st BPC Sl 1 st to cn and hold to *back*, k1tbl, p1 from cn.
2-st FPC Sl 1 st to cn and hold to *front*, p1, k1tbl from cn.
3-st BC Sl 1 st to cn and hold to *back*, k2, k1 from cn.
3-st FC Sl 2 sts to cn and hold to *front*, k1, k2 from cn.
3-st BPC Sl 1 st to cn and hold to *back,* k2, p1 from cn.
3-st FPC Sl 2 sts to cn and hold to *front*, p1, k2 from cn.
4-st FC Sl 2 sts to cn and hold to *front*, k2, k2 from cn.
6-st BC Sl 3 sts to cn and hold to *back*, k3, k3 from cn.
6-st FC Sl 3 sts to cn and hold to *front*, k3, k3 from cn.

HAT

Cast on 62 sts.
Row 1 (RS) *K2, p2; rep from *, end k2.

Row 2 *P2, k2; rep from *, end p2. Rep rows 1 and 2 for k2, p2 rib until piece measures 4½"/11.5cm from beg, inc 8 sts evenly across last WS row—70 sts.

Beg charts

Row 1 (RS) Work seed st over 13 sts, p2, k1tbl, p2, work row 1 of cable chart A over next 6 sts, p2, k1tbl, work row 1 of diamond chart over next 16 sts, k1tbl, p2, work row 1 of cable chart B over next 6 sts, p2, k1tbl, p2, work seed st over 13 sts.

Row 2 Work seed st over 13 sts, k2, p1tbl, k2, work row 2 of cable chart B over next 6 sts, k2, p1tbl, work row 2 of diamond chart over next 16 sts, p1tbl, k2, work row 2 of cable chart A over next 6 sts, k2, p1tbl, k2, work seed st over 13 sts. Cont in pats as established through diamond chart row 22, then work rows 1 and 2 once more.

Shape top

Row 1 (RS) P1, k1, [p3tog, k1] twice, p3tog, p2tog, k1tbl, p2tog, k6, p2tog, k1tbl, p2tog, work next 12 sts in diamond pat, p2tog, k1tbl, p2tog, k6,

p2tog, k1tbl, p2tog, [p3tog, k1] 3 times, p1—50 sts. Work 1 row even.

Row 3 [P1, k1] 3 times, p2, k1tbl, p1, 6-st BC, p1, k1tbl, p2tog, work next 10 sts in diamond pat, p2tog, k1tbl, p1, 6-st FC, p1, k1tbl, p2, [k1, p1] 3 times—48 sts.

Row 4 [P1, k1] 4 times, p1tbl, k1, [p2tog] 3 times, k1, p1tbl, k2, p1tbl, p2tog, p1, k1, p2tog, p1tbl, k2, p1tbl, k1, [p2tog] 3 times, k1, p1tbl, [k1, p1] 4 times—40 sts.

Row 5 P1, k1, p3tog, k1, p2, k1tbl, p1, k3, p1, k1tbl, p2tog, k2tog, k1, p1, k2tog, p2tog, k1tbl, p1, k3, p1, k1tbl, p2, k1, p3tog, k1, p1—32 sts.

Row 6 [P1, k1] 3 times, p1tbl, k1, p3tog, k1, p1tbl, k1, [p2tog] twice, k1, p1tbl, k1, p3tog, k1, p1tbl, [k1, p1] 3 times—26 sts.

Cut yarn, leave a long end. Draw through rem sts and fasten tightly.

FINISHING

Sew center back seam, reversing seam for turnback cuff. Make a 4"/10cm pompom and attach to top of hat. ■

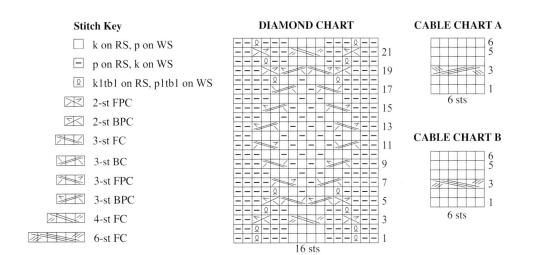

Stitch Key

☐ k on RS, p on WS

⊟ p on RS, k on WS

Ⴒ k1tb1 on RS, p1tb1 on WS

2-st FPC

2-st BPC

3-st FC

3-st BC

3-st FPC

3-st BPC

4-st FC

6-st FC

DIAMOND CHART

21 19 17 15 13 11 9 7 5 3 1

16 sts

CABLE CHART A

6 5 3 1

6 sts

CABLE CHART B

6 5 3 1

6 sts

Bobbled Visor Hat

With a practical visor to keep the sun and snow out of your eyes, pretty Fair Isle patterning, and perky bobbles, Jacqueline van Dillen's fun-loving hat will be the talk of the slopes.

SIZE
Instructions are written for one size.

KNITTED MEASUREMENTS
Circumference approx 24"/61cm
Length approx 10½"/26.5cm

MATERIALS
• 2 3½oz/100g hanks (each approx 164yd/150m) of Cascade Yarns *Eco Cloud* (undyed merino wool/undyed alpaca) in #1802 cream (MC) (5)

• 1 3½oz/100g hank (each approx 164yd/150m) of Cascade Yarns *Cloud* (merino wool/baby alpaca) each in #2120 royal (A) and #2121 light blue (B) (5)

• One pair size 9 (5.5mm) needles OR SIZE TO OBTAIN GAUGE

• One 7" x 8"/18cm x 20.5cm heavy-duty stencil blank, or two 7" x 8"/18cm x 20.5cm medium-weight stencil blanks

• Black fine-tip permanent marker

GAUGE
18 sts and 24 rows = 4"/10cm over St st using size 9 (5.5mm) needles.
TAKE TIME TO CHECK GAUGE.

STITCH GLOSSARY

Make bobble In same st, work: k1, [p1, k1] twice, making 5 sts from one; turn. P5, turn. K5, turn. P5, turn. Working one stitch at a time, pass 5th st on LH needle over first st on LH needle, then 4th st, 3rd st, then 2nd st over first st. Place st on RH needle.

K2, P2 RIB
(multiple of 4 sts plus 2)
Row 1 (RS) K2, *p2, k2; rep from * to end.
Row 2 P2, *k2, p2; rep from * to end.
Rep rows 1 and 2 for k2, p2 rib.

HAT
Cuff
With MC, cast on 114 sts. Work in k2, p2 rib for 5"/12.5cm, end with a WS row. Cont in St st (knit on RS, purl on WS) and work even for 4 rows.
Bobble row 1 (RS) With MC, k2, *with A, make bobble, with MC, k5; rep from *, end with A, make bobble, with MC, k3. Cut A. With MC and beg with a purl row, cont in St st for 3 rows, end with a WS row.

Beg chart pat
Row 1 (RS) Work first st, work 16-st rep 7 times, work last st. Cont to foll chart in this way to row 13. Cut B. With MC and beg with a purl row, cont in St st for 3 rows, end with a WS row.

Bobble row 2 (RS) Rep bobble row 1. Cut A. With MC only and beg with a purl row, cont in St st for 1 row, end with a WS row.

Crown shaping

Dec row 1 (RS) K1, *k14, ssk; rep from *, end k1—107 sts. Purl next row.

Dec row 2 (RS) K1, *k13, ssk; rep from *, end k1—100 sts. Purl next row.

Dec row 3 (RS) K1, *k12, ssk; rep from *, end k1—93 sts. Purl next row.

Dec row 4 (RS) K1, *k11, ssk; rep from *, end k1—86 sts. Purl next row.

Dec row 5 (RS) K1, *k10, ssk; rep from *, end k1—79 sts. Purl next row.

Dec row 6 (RS) K1, *k9, ssk; rep from *, end k1—72 sts. Purl next row.

Dec row 7 (RS) K1, *k8, ssk; rep from *, end k1—65 sts. Purl next row.

Dec row 8 (RS) K1, *k7, ssk; rep from *, end k1—58 sts. Purl next row.

Dec row 9 (RS) K1, *k6, ssk; rep from *, end k1—51 sts. Purl next row.

Dec row 10 (RS) K1, *k5, ssk; rep from *, end k1—44 sts. Purl next row.

Dec row 11 (RS) K1, *k4, ssk; rep from *, end k1—37 sts. Purl next row.

Dec row 12 (RS) K1, *k3, ssk; rep from *, end k1—30 sts. Purl next row.

Dec row 13 (RS) K1, *k2, ssk; rep from *, end k1—23 sts. Purl next row.

Dec row 14 (RS) K1, *k1, ssk; rep from *, end k1—16 sts. Purl next row.

Dec row 15 (RS) K1, *ssk; rep from *, end k1—9 sts.

Dec row 16 (WS) [P2tog] 4 times, p1—5 sts. Cut yarn, leaving a 20"/51cm tail, and thread through rem sts. Pull tog tightly and secure end, then sew back seam, reversing seam over last 2½"/6.5cm.

FINISHING

Enlarge template to 100 percent on photocopier. Using marker, trace one actual-size visor from heavy-weight stencil blank, or two from medium-weight blanks. Cut out. On RS of hat, position visor at center front. Fold ribbed band over to RS and wrap and stretch band over visor, so cast-on edge is even with last row of rib; pin in place. Continue to wrap and pin ribbed band in this way around entire hat. Using MC, whipstitch cast-on edge in place. ■

VISOR TEMPLATE
(shown at 90%)

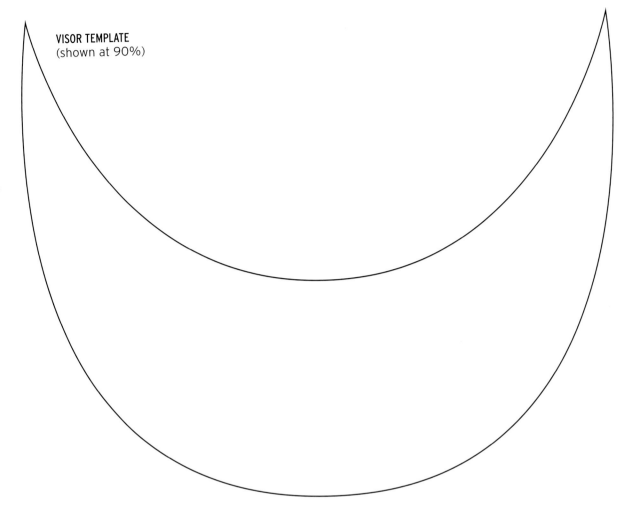

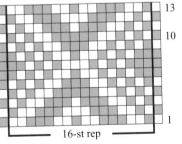

13

10

1

16-st rep

Color Key

☐ Cream (MC)

▨ Light blue (B)

Feathered Fascinator

Perfect for a royal wedding or just a glamorous evening out,
Linda Medina's embellished fascinator puts the (British) accent on style.

SIZE

Instructions are written for one size.

KNITTED MEASUREMENTS

Flower approx 4¼"/11cm x 4¼"/11cm
Finished fascinator (excluding feathers) approx
9"/23cm wide x 10"/25.5cm high

MATERIALS

• 1 1¾oz/50g hank (each approx 75yd/69m)
of Trendsetter *Zoe* (cotton/viscose/polyester) in
#1 mushroom soup (**4**)

• One pair size 8 (5mm) needles
OR SIZE TO OBTAIN GAUGE

• One 1½"/4cm wide x 4"/10cm long
metal hair comb in black

• 1¼ yd/1.25m of 1½"/38mm-wide sheer
ribbon in mocha

• 1¾yd/1.75m of 9"/23cm-wide
millinery netting in black with ⅜"/1cm-diameter
chenille dots

• Four 8"/20.5cm-long trimmed coque
feathers in black

• Sewing thread in black

• Buttonhole thread in black

• Size 13 chenille needle

• Sewing needle

• Straight pins

• Designer tacky glue

GAUGE

16 sts and 18 rows = 4"/10cm in St st using size 8
(5mm) needles. TAKE TIME TO CHECK GAUGE.

STITCH GLOSSARY

kfb Inc 1 by knitting into the front and
back of the next st.

FLOWER

Cast on 5 sts. Cont in St st (knit on RS,
purl on WS) and work even for 2 rows.
Shape one side edge as foll:
Next (inc) row (RS) Kfb, knit to end—6 sts. Purl next
row. Rep last 2 rows six times more—12 sts.
Work even until piece measures 29"/73.5cm from
beg (measured along straight edge), end
with a WS row.
Next (dec) row (RS) K2tog, knit to end—11 sts.
Purl next row. Rep last 2 rows 6 times more—5
sts. Work even for 2 rows. Bind off, leaving
a long tail for sewing.

FINISHING

Flower

Thread tail into yarn needle. Sew running stitch
along curved edge. Draw up tightly to gather. Fold

curved corner over and stitch at gathered edge to secure for center of flower. Continue rolling and twisting strip into flower shape, securing with stitches at base. Fold the curved end back on itself and secure with a few stitches to finish off. End off yarn on WS of flower.

Bow

Leaving a 6"/15cm-long tail, make four 3½"/9cm-long loops, arranged side-by-side. With sewing thread doubled in sewing needle, make running stitches through base of each loop and gather slightly. Make back stitches to secure thread. Trim second tail to 6"/15cm long. Trim both tails on an angle. Pin bow to back of flower. Have inner edges of ribbon ends 6"/15cm apart. Position loops so they are spaced 1"/2.5cm from tail at left and 3"/7.5cm from tail at right. Use buttonhole thread and chenille needle to whipstitch base of bow to flower; remove pins.

Netting

Leaving a 6"/15cm-long tail, make four 5"/12.5cm-long loops. Wrap base of each loop with sewing thread doubled. Use sewing needle to make back stitches to secure thread. Trim second tail to 6"/15cm long. Pin netting to back of flower over bow. Align netting tails under ribbon tails. Arrange netting loops evenly between tails. Trim both tails on an angle. Use buttonhole thread and chenille needle to whipstitch base of netting to flower; remove pins.

Hair comb

Position comb so curved side is away from you. Position fascinator on comb, so bow is at upper left. Use buttonhole thread and chenille needle and whipstitch comb through netting, bow, and upper layer of flower.

Coque feathers

Insert cut end of each feather into flower. Have the feathers angling forward and placed immediately in front of the bow or netting. Remove each, then dip ½"/1.5cm of cut end into glue and insert back into same location in flower; let dry. ■

Beaded Bucket Hat

Ahoy! You're ready to set sail when you don Lois S. Young's nautical-inspired bucket hat. The blue-as-the-sea beads are added with a crochet hook as you knit.

SIZE

Instructions are written for one size.

KNITTED MEASUREMENTS

Circumference approx 22"/56cm
Length approx 8½"/21.5cm

MATERIALS

• 2 3½oz/100g skeins (each approx 210yd/193m) Berroco *Comfort* (super fine nylon/acrylic) in #9702 pearl (4)

• One size 8 (5mm) circular needle, 16"/40cm long, OR SIZE TO OBTAIN GAUGE

• One set (5) size 8 (5mm) double-pointed needles (dpns)

• Size D/3 (3.25mm) crochet hook

• 2 bags (100 beads per bag) of 9 x 7mm glass crow beads in translucent cobalt blue

• Stitch marker

GAUGE

16 sts and 40 rnds = 4"/10cm over garter st using size 8 (5mm) needle.
TAKE TIME TO CHECK GAUGE.

NOTE

Crown of hat is worked from the bottom up, then brim is picked up and worked from the crown down.

STITCH GLOSSARY

AB (add bead) Insert crochet hook through bead, then use hook to remove next st from LH needle. Use hook to draw st through bead, then place st on RH needle without working it.

HAT

Crown

With circular needle, cast on 90 sts loosely. Join and pm, taking care not to twist sts on needle.

Rnds 1, 3, and 5 Purl.

Rnds 2 and 4 Knit.

Rnd 6 *K5, AB, k4; rep from * around. Rep rnds 1–6 four times more.

Crown shaping

Change to dpns (dividing sts evenly among 4 needles) when there are too few sts on circular needle.

Rnd 1 Purl.

Rnd 2 (dec) *K3, ssk, k5; rep from * around—81 sts.

Rnd 3 Purl.

Rnd 4 Knit.

Rnd 5 Purl.

Rnd 6 *K4, AB, k4; rep from * around.

Rnd 7 Purl.

Rnd 8 (dec) *K5, k2tog, k2; rep from * around—72 sts.

Rnd 9 Purl.

Rnd 10 Knit.

Rnd 11 Purl.

Rnd 12 (dec) *K2, ssk, AB, k3; rep from * around—63 sts.

Rnd 13 Purl.

Rnd 14 Knit.

Rnd 15 Purl.

Rnd 16 (dec) *K4, k2tog, k1; rep from * around—54 sts.

Rnd 17 Purl.

Rnd 18 *K2, AB, k3; rep from * around.

Rnd 19 Purl.

Rnd 20 (dec) *Ssk, k2, k2tog; rep from * around—36 sts.

Rnd 21 Purl.

Rnd 22 (dec) *S2KP, k1; rep from * around—18 sts.

Rnd 23 (dec) [P2tog] 9 times—9 sts. Cut yarn, leaving an 8"/20.5cm tail, and thread through rem sts. Thread on a bead, then pull tog tightly and secure end.

Brim

With RS facing and circular needle, pick up and k 90 sts around bottom edge. Join, and pm for beg of rnds.

Rnd 1 Purl.

Rnd 2 (inc) *K3, M1; rep from * around—120 sts.

Rnds 3 and 5 Purl.

Rnds 4 and 6 Knit.

Rnd 7 Purl.

Rnd 8 *K3, AB, k2; rep from * around.

Rnd 9 Purl.

Rnd 10 Knit.

Rnd 11 Purl.

Rnd 12 (inc) *K3, M1, k3; rep from * around—140 sts.

Rnd 13 Purl.

Rnd 14 *K3, AB, k3; rep from * around.

Rnds 15, 17, and 19 Purl.

Rnds 16, 18, and 20 Knit.

Rnd 21 Purl. Bind off loosely purlwise. ∎

Tasseled Chullo

Erssie Major blends traditions with a Peruvian-style hat that features Native American and Aztec motifs.

SIZE

Instructions are written for one size.

KNITTED MEASUREMENTS

Circumference approx 19½"/49.5cm

Length (excluding earflaps) approx 8¾"/22cm

MATERIALS

• 1 1¾oz/50g hank (each approx 109yd/100m) of Classic Elite *Inca Alpaca* (baby alpaca) each in #1198 persimmon (MC) and #1142 cajamaica maroon (CC) (**4**)

• One size 7 (4.5mm) circular needle, 16"/40cm long, OR SIZE TO OBTAIN GAUGE

• One set (5) size 7 (4.5mm) double-pointed needles (dpns)

• Size G/6 (4mm) crochet hook

• Stitch marker

• Removeable stitch markers or small safety pins

• Buttonhole thread (any color)

• Sewing needle

GAUGE

20 sts and 24 rnds = 4"/10cm over chart pats using size 7 (4.5mm) needle.
TAKE TIME TO CHECK GAUGE.

NOTES

1) Hat section of chullo is worked first, then earflaps are added after.

2) Charts 1–3 of hat section are worked in the rnd. Read charts from right to left.

3) Chart 4 (earflap) is worked back and forth. Read odd (RS) rows from right to left and even (WS) rows from left to right.

CHULLO

With circular needle and MC, cast on 96 sts. Join and pm, taking care not to twist sts on needle. Cont in garter st ridge as foll:

Next rnd Knit

Next rnd Purl. Cont in St st (knit every rnd) and work as foll:

Beg chart pat 1

Rnd 1 (RS) Work 6-st rep 16 times. Cont to foll chart in this way through rnd 5.

Next rnd With MC, knit.

Next rnd With CC, knit.

Beg chart pat 2

Rnd 1 (RS) Work sts 1–55 once, then sts 1–41 once. Cont to foll chart in this way through rnd 20.

Next rnd With CC, knit.

Next rnd With MC, knit.

Beg chart pat 3

Rnd 1 (RS) Work 6-st rep 16 times. Cont to foll chart in this way through rnd 5.

Next rnd With MC, knit.

Next rnd With CC, knit.

Next rnd With MC, knit.

Next 3 rnds With CC, knit.

Crown shaping

Change to dpns (dividing sts evenly among 4 needles) when there are too few sts on circular needle. Cont to work with CC only as foll:

Dec rnd 1 *K10, k2tog; rep from * around—88 sts.

Dec rnd 2 *K9, k2tog; rep from * around—80 sts.

Dec rnd 3 *K8, k2tog; rep from * around—72 sts.

Dec rnd 4 *K7, k2tog; rep from * around—64 sts.

Dec rnd 5 *K6, k2tog; rep from * around—56 sts.

Dec rnd 6 *K5, k2tog; rep from * around—48 sts.

Dec rnd 7 *K4, k2tog; rep from * around—40 sts.

Dec rnd 8 *K3, k2tog; rep from * around—32 sts.

Dec rnd 9 *K2, k2tog; rep from * around—24 sts.

Dec rnd 10 *K1, k2tog; rep from * around—16 sts.

Dec rnd 11 [K2tog] 8 times—8 sts. Cut CC, leaving an 8"/20.5cm tail, and thread through rem sts.

Right earflap

With RS facing and bottom edge of hat section facing up, place a removeable marker between first st and last st of joined rnd. Count 9 sts to the left of marker. With RS facing, dpns and CC, and beg in 10th st, pick up and k 1 st in each of next 25 sts.

Beg chart pat 4

Row 2 (WS) P25. Cont with row 3, work chart in this way through row 24, working dec's as indicated—3 sts. Cut CC. Change to MC.

I-cord tie

Work in I-cord as foll: ***Next row (RS)** With 2nd dpn, k3, do not turn. Slide sts back to beg of needle to work next row from RS; rep from * until I-cord measures 7½"/19cm from beg. Cut yarn, leaving a 10"/25.5cm tail. Thread tail into tapestry needle,

then thread through rem sts. Pull tog tightly and secure end. Leave tail.

Left earflap

With RS facing and bottom edge of hat section facing up, count 8 sts to the right of center marker; place a removeable marker in 9th st. Count 25 sts to the right of last marker; place a removeable marker in 26th st. With RS facing, dpns and CC, pick up and k 25 sts between markers. Cont to work as for right earflap. Remove markers.

FINISHING

Steam lightly to even out stitches.

Edging

With RS facing, crochet hook, and CC, join yarn with a sl st in center back edge. **Rnd 1 (RS)** Ch 1, sc in each st around, working 2 sc in front of each earflap tie, join rnd with a sl st in first sc, changing to MC. Cut CC. **Rnd 2 (RS)** Ch 1, sc in each st around, join rnd with a sl st in first st.

Fasten off. Tack down crochet edge around tips of earflaps to neaten.

Tassels for I-cord ties (make 2)

Make a 3½"/9cm-long tassel using CC. Sew tassel to I-cord tie using tail from tie.

Two-color twisted cord

Cut three 18"/46cm lengths of MC and CC. Gather each color group together with an overhand knot in one end. Keeping the strands of equal length and straight, make an overhand knot in the other end of each group. Trim yarn ends to ⅜"/1cm. Butt a MC knotted end with a CC knotted end. Sew together using a double strand of thread. Cut a 6"/15cm length of any color yarn. Knot it above one of the end knots, then tie it to a hook to secure. Insert pencil above last end knot. Rotate pencil clockwise until yarn is so tight it starts to twist back onto itself. Each 3-strand yarn group will twist together and appear as 1 strand. Fold in half by holding strand where knots are butted and sewn. Hold end with pencil to loop over hook. Release halfway point and allow yarn to twist on itself. Tie loose ends together with an overhand knot.

Tassel for two-color twisted cord

Using MC, make a 2½"/6.5cm-long tassel, inserting strands between twisted cord to hide overhand knot. Using MC, wrap tassel ¾"/2cm below top of tassel. Insert opposite end of twisted cord through opening in crown. Use CC tail to pull sts tog tightly and secure end

CHART 1

5

1

6-st rep

CHART 3

5

1

6-st rep

Color Key

- ▨ Persimmon (MC)
- ■ Cajamaica maroon (CC)

Stitch Key

- ☐ k every rnd (charts 1–3)
- ☐ k on RS, p on WS (chart 4)
- ▨ no stitch
- ◩ k2tog
- ◪ ssk
- ⟑ S2KP

CHART 4

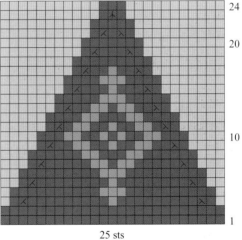

24

20

10

1

25 sts

CHART 2

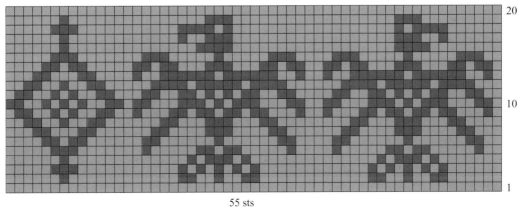

20

10

1

55 sts

Helpful Information

Abbreviations

approx	approximately
beg	begin(ning)
CC	contrasting color
ch	chain
cm	centimeter(s)
cn	cable needle
cont	continu(e)(ing)
dec	decreas(e)(ing)
dpn	double-pointed needle(s)
foll	follow(s)(ing)
g	gram(s)
inc	increas(e)(ing)
k	knit
k2tog	knit 2 sts tog (one st has been decreased)
LH	left-hand
lp(s)	loop(s)
m	meter(s)
mm	millimeter(s)
MC	main color
M1	make one st; with needle tip, lift strand between last st knit and next st on LH needle and knit into back of it
M1 p-st	make 1 purl st
oz	ounce(s)
p	purl
pat(s)	pattern(s)
pm	place marker
psso	pass slip stitch(es) over
rem	remain(s)(ing)
rep	repeat
RH	right-hand
RS	right side(s)
rnd(s)	round(s)

SKP	slip 1, knit 1, pass slip st over (one st has been decreased)
SK2P	slip 1, knit 2 tog, pass slip st over the knit 2 tog (two sts have been decreased)
S2KP	slip 2 sts tog, knit 1, pass 2 slip sts over knit 1 (two sts have been decreased)
sl	slip
sl st	slip stitch
ssk	slip 2 sts kwise, one at a time; insert tip of LH needle into front of these sts and knit them tog (one st has been decreased)
sssk	slip 3 sts kwise, one at a time; insert tip of LH needle into front of these sts and knit them tog (two sts have been decreased)
st(s)	stitch(es)
St st	stockinette stitch
tbl	through back loop(s)
tog	together
WS	wrong side(s)
wyib	with yarn in back
wyif	with yarn in front
yd	yard(s)
yo	yarn over needle
*	repeat directions following*
[ ]	repeat directions inside brackets as many times as indicated

Knitting Needles

U.S.	METRIC
0	2mm
1	2.25mm
2	2.75mm
3	3.25mm
4	3.5mm
5	3.75mm
6	4mm
7	4.5mm
8	5mm
9	5.5mm
10	6mm
10½	6.5mm
11	8mm
13	9mm
15	10mm
17	12.75mm
19	15mm
35	19mm

Skill Levels

1. BEGINNER
Ideal first project.

2. EASY
Basic stitches, minimal shaping, and simple finishing.

3. INTERMEDIATE
For knitters with some experience. More intricate stitches, shaping, and finishing.

4. EXPERIENCED
For knitters able to work patterns with complicated shaping and finishing.

Yarn Substitutions

The yarns for several of the patterns originally published in *Vogue Knitting* have been discontinued. These are the original yarns:

TUQUE (page 36)
• Two .88oz/25g hanks (each approx 88yd/80m) of Knit One Crochet Too *USDK* (wool) each in #675 navy (A) and #613 blueberry (pale blue B) (4)
• 1 hank each in #272 wine (C), #574 ivy (D), #757 twilight (purple E), and #913 granite (F)

CHULLO (page 52)
• 1 1½ oz/50g skein (each approx 93yd/85m) of Nashua Handknits/ Westminster Fibers, Inc., *Julia* (wool/alpaca/mohair) each in #6085 geranium (A), #2163 golden honey (B), #3961 lady's mantle (C), #3158 purple basil (D), #121 persimmon (E), #8141 pretty pink (F), and #6086 velvet moss (G) (4)

CABLED TAM (page 60)
• 3 1½ oz/50g balls (each approx 126yd/115m) of Filatura di Crosa/Tahki·Stacy Charles, Inc. *Wave* (wool/silk) in #3 beige (4)

LEAF LACE BERET (page 100)
• 2 1¾ oz/50g hanks (each approx 165yd/151m) of Tilli Tomas *Milan* (cashmere/silk/merino) in #20S whisper (1)

RIDGED BERET (page 148)
• 1 (2) 1¾ oz/50g skeins (each approx 146yd/134m) of Misti Alpaca *Sport* (baby alpaca) each in #NT505 natural grey (A) and #2081 chocolate caramel moulinette (B) (1)

Resources

Alpaca With A Twist
950 S. White River Pkwy W Dr.
Indianapolis, IN 46221
www.alpacawithatwist.com

Bergère de France North America
100 Blvd Marie Victorin
Boucherville, QC J4B 1V6
Canada
www.bergeredefrance.com

Berroco, Inc.
1 Tupperware Drive, Suite 4
North Smithfield, RI 02896-6815
www.berroco.com

Blue Sky Alpacas
P.O. Box 88
Cedar, MN 55011
www.blueskyalpacas.com

Brown Sheep Company
100662 County Road 16
Mitchell, Nebraska 69357
www.brownsheep.com

Cascade Yarns
1224 Andover Park East
Tukwila, WA 98188
www.cascadeyarns.com

Classic Elite Yarns
16 Esquire Road, Unit 2
N. Billerica, MA 01862
www.classiceliteyarns.com

Crystal Palace Yarns
160 23rd Street
Richmond, CA 94804
www.crystalpalaceyarns.com

Debbie Bliss
Distributed by KFI

Filatura di Crosa
Distributed by Tahki·Stacy
Charles, Inc.

Fyberspates Ltd.
In the U.S.: Distributed by
Lantern Moon
In the UK:
Unit 6, Oxleaze Farm Workshops
Broughton Poggs
Filkins
Lechlade
Glos, GL7 3RB
United Kingdom

Jade Sapphire Exotic Fibres
www.jadesapphire.com

KFI
P.O. Box 336
315 Bayview Avenue
Amityville, NY 11701
www.knittingfever.com

Knit One, Crochet Too
91 Tandberg Trail, Unit 6
Windham, ME 04062
www.knitonecrochettoo.com

Koigu Wool Designs
P.O. Box 158
Chatsworth, ON N0H 1G0
Canada
www.koigu.com

Lantern Moon
7911 NE 33rd Drive
Suite 140
Portland, OR 97211 US
www.lanternmoon.com

Lopi
Distributed by
Westminster Fibers

Louet North America
808 Commerce Park Drive
Ogdensburg, NY 13669
www.louet.com

Louisa Harding
Distributed by KFI

Misti Alpaca Yarns
In the U.S.:
P.O. Box 2532
Glen Ellyn, Illinois 60138
www.mistialpaca.com
In Canada:
Distributed by the Old Mill
Knitting Company

Noro
Distributed by KFI

Old Mill Knitting Company
F.G. P.O. Box 81176
Ancaster, Ontario L9G 4X2
www.oldmillknitting.com

Plymouth Yarn Co.
500 Lafayette Street
Bristol, PA 19007
www.plymouthyarn.com

Rowan
Distributed by
Westminster Fibers

Shibui Knits, LLC.
1500 NW 18th Suite 110
Portland, OR 97209
info@shibuiknits.com

Tahki Yarns
Distributed by Tahki·Stacy
Charles, Inc.

Tahki·Stacy Charles, Inc.
70-60 83rd Street, Building 12
Glendale, NY 11385
www.tahkistacycharles.com

Tilli Tomas
Tel: (617) 524-3330
www.tillitomas.com

Trendsetter Yarns
In the U.S.:
16745 Saticoy Street, Suite 101
Van Nuys, CA 91406
www.trendsetteryarns.com
In Canada: Distributed by the
Old Mill Knitting Company

Universal Yarn
284 Ann Street
Concord, NC 28025
www.universalyarn.com

Westminster Fibers
8 Shelter Drive
Greer, SC 29650
www.westminsterfibers.com

Standard Yarn Weight System

Categories of yarn, gauge ranges, and recommended needle and hook sizes

Yarn Weight Symbol & Category Names	0 Lace	1 Super Fine	2 Fine	3 Light	4 Medium	5 Bulky	6 Super Bulky
Type of Yarns in Category	Fingering 10 count crochet thread	Sock, Fingering, Baby	Sport, Baby	DK, Light Worsted	Worsted, Afghan, Aran	Chunky, Craft, Rug	Bulky, Roving
Knit Gauge Range* in Stockinette Stitch to 4 inches	33–40** sts	27–32 sts	23–26 sts	21–24 sts	16–20 sts	12–15 sts	6–11 sts
Recommended Needle in Metric Size Range	1.5–2.25 mm	2.25–3.25 mm	3.25–3.75 mm	3.75–4.5 mm	4.5–5.5 mm	5.5–8 mm	8 mm and larger
Recommended Needle U.S. Size Range	000 to 1	1 to 3	3 to 5	5 to 7	7 to 9	9 to 11	11 and larger
Crochet Gauge* Ranges in Single Crochet to 4 inch	32–42 double crochets**	21–32 sts	16–20 sts	12–17 sts	11–14 sts	8–11 sts	5–9 sts
Recommended Hook in Metric Size Range	Steel*** 1.6–1.4mm Regular hook 2.25 mm	2.25–3.5 mm	3.5–4.5 mm	4.5–5.5 mm	5.5–6.5 mm	6.5–9 mm	9 mm and larger
Recommended Hook U.S. Size Range	Steel*** 6, 7, 8 Regular hook B–1	B/1 to E/4	E/4 to 7	7 to I/9	I/9 to K/10½	K/10½ to M/13	M/13 and larger

* GUIDELINES ONLY: The above reflect the most commonly used gauges and needle or hook sizes for specific yarn categories.

** Lace weight yarns are usually knitted or crocheted on larger needles and hooks to create lacy, openwork patterns. Accordingly, a gauge range is difficult to determine. Always follow the gauge stated in your pattern.

*** Steel crochet hooks are sized differently from regular hooks--the higher the number, the smaller the hook, which is the reverse of regular hook sizing.

This Standards & Guidelines booklet and downloadable symbol artwork are available at: **YarnStandards.com**

Index